DON'T
STOP
DANCING

◆ ◆ ◆ ◆ ◆ ◆ ◆ ◆

MY STORY OF TRAGEDY,
LOSS, ADDICTION, AND DARKNESS
AND THE DISCOVERY THAT HEALED MY SOUL

ERIC ANDERSON

TABLE OF CONTENTS

◆ ◆ ◆ ◆ ◆ ◆ ◆ ◆ ◆

I

◆ ◆ ◆ ◆ ◆ ◆ ◆ ◆ ◆

IN A PERFECT WORLD

CHAPTER ONE

◆ ◆ ◆ ◆ ◆ ◆ ◆ ◆ ◆

Growing Pains

I REMEMBER LIKE IT WAS yesterday. Growing up as a little kid in Fort Worth, Texas, in the 80s, I loved playing soccer more so than football, despite the fact that football is often the more popular sport in Texas. My coach would instruct my teammates whenever they got the ball to kick it up field, past the defense, and let me do the rest. I would outrun every player to the ball and break away to the goal, where it would be just me against the goalie. I was the fastest kid on the field every game. Nobody could catch me!

The same applied to other sports and activities I participated in. The coaches made a concerted effort to ensure the ball was in my hands as often as possible. I was a gifted athlete and usually better than anybody else on the court or field during games. I liked being the best. Even more, I liked all the attention it brought.

One day, I was riding home in the car with my father after scoring seven goals in a soccer game. I was basking in the glory, and my dad could sense a bit of arrogance. Usually, I would be rewarded with praise and ice cream, but not that day. Instead, my dad decided to turn my success into a valuable life lesson. As we drove home on that hot summer day, he turned off the radio and cut me off as I bragged about my stellar performance.

"Son, you can be the most athletic, most popular, best-looking kid in the world, and none of it matters if you waste your talent," he told me.

"What do you mean, Dad?" I asked, confused.

"What I mean is, scoring seven goals, being better than everybody else, none of it matters if you don't do anything with it. Don't waste your talent!"

My father's advice and lesson for life went in one ear and out the other. I was young and not looking at the big picture. All I wanted was to be the best player on the field every game. I wanted all the attention and accolades. I liked winning, and I liked putting on a show. More importantly, I wanted to make my mom and dad proud of me. While we resided in Texas, I had all of this—at school, in my neighborhood, on the playing field, and at home.

That's why the move to California was such a difficult transition. My dad had different jobs that took us from Minnesota, where I was born, to Indiana, Texas, and now California. I grew up in Texas, though, and for me that was home. That's where all my friends were, that's where I stood out, and that's where my sister chose to remain. My other sister was still in Minnesota.

Both of my sisters were from my parents' previous marriages, and both were older than me. I guess they didn't enjoy all the moving, something I was too young to comprehend at first. Now that I was older, I understood why they didn't come along—at least, I thought I did. I'm sure my two sisters' relationships with my mom and dad were more complex than just moving, but I never saw that aspect as a child. My only memories of them at that stage were of them dressing me up as a girl and putting makeup on me, something they claim I thoroughly enjoyed, but I still dispute this.

I wished my sisters had moved with us to California, though, because that state was not very welcoming to a Southern boy from Texas. I couldn't play any sports because we moved around quite a bit when we first landed in the Golden State. When my family finally settled in San Diego, I hated going to school. The other students picked on me because of my accent, and I got into a lot of fights.

I wasn't used to that type of negative attention. In Texas, I was the bully. I was the one teasing other kids and pulling their underwear up over their heads. In California, I had to defend myself every day from that type of torment. Funny how the tables had turned—maybe it was karma? Regardless, I felt so alone. I remember playing by myself constantly, and my only friends were imaginary.

With no organized sports to play and no friends to hang out with, I found my refuge down in San Diego Bay. That's where I first discovered music and dancing. Groups of guys with their boomboxes and cardboard cutouts would be breakdancing in the harbor for all of the tourists. They would battle dance to hip-hop music blaring from the speakers. It was the coolest shit I'd ever seen.

I started spending so much time in San Diego Bay that some of the guys took me under their wing and taught me to breakdance. I began making mixtapes at home and would practice dancing in front of the mirror. Every chance I had to go down to the bay and dance, I would take it. It was my escape from the constant bullying, and breakdancing became my new sport in California.

We weren't in California long, though—less than two years. My dad's job took us back to Fort Worth, Texas. I didn't mind moving back. California had chewed me up and spit me out. It was a different culture from what I had grown up around in Texas. The only good things about the move to San Diego were the ocean, the beautiful weather, and my newfound love and appreciation for music and dancing.

In Texas, I returned to my old school in Fort Worth, and it was like I had returned from the dead. None of my former classmates could believe I was back. It made me more popular than ever, and it felt great to have returned. I had all my old friends back, started playing sports again, and—best of all—I introduced my classmates to a thing called breakdancing.

In music class, our teacher held a talent contest every week, so I formed a breakdancing crew called Captain Crunch & the Funky Bunch. My friends and I practiced in our garages after school and on the weekends. We laid down cardboard on the concrete, and I showed them how to do the worm and backspin. Those country kids had never seen anything like that, and they loved it.

I was riding a wave of unprecedented popularity as I entered junior high. Breakdancing faded away, so naturally, sports took up most of my time. I concentrated on soccer and football, and my dominance on the field continued. I also became very interested in girls and refined my skills in chivalry. I had everything a kid in school could want.

It's astounding how much easier getting an education is when you're good-looking, athletic, and popular. That's why, when I moved back to Texas, I stopped picking on other kids like I used to do. I remembered what I had gone through in California, and I didn't want other kids to suffer through that same harassment. Some kids had it rough in class, and I tried to intervene whenever I saw somebody getting bullied.

Just when things were going great, though, my dad lost his job, and we had to move back to Minnesota. The move virtually neutered my athletic ability, and my popularity along with it. Minnesota was a hockey state, and the only ice in Texas was found in freezers. I soon realized nobody cared about soccer or football, and subsequently, nobody cared about me. I tried lacing up the hockey skates, but I was like a newborn deer trying to walk on a frozen lake.

Worse yet, the embarrassing stages of puberty were beginning to take hold. My voice changed, and I started to develop acne. I was no longer the popular jock I had been in Texas. Now I was irrelevant and ignored. I was picked on for my southern accent just like in California. I had a few friends and played on the soccer team, but it wasn't the stardom I had become accustomed to. I felt isolated, and school wasn't fun anymore.

Once summer came, I started caddying at the White Bear Yacht Club, named after the town I lived in and the big lake nearby. That's where I found my new refuge, just like I had in San Diego Bay. Instead of breakdancing, though, I discovered golf. It was one of the perks of working there as a caddy. On certain days, during certain hours, the caddies got to play as much golf as we wanted. So that's what I did all summer—caddied and golfed.

Just like dancing and music had given me a special feeling of serenity, so did being on the golf course. Spending time out there in nature, with all the trees, birds, and squirrels, brought me peace. It was a quiet escape from all the pressure that came with being a teenager. I didn't have to act a certain way to avoid getting teased; I could just relax and concentrate on my swing. My interest in golf grew, and I even started playing with my dad.

I kept this up through my sophomore year of high school because I was making friends at the country club, doing side jobs for some members, and earning good money. Some of the hockey players worked there during the summer, and I started playing golf with them after we were all done with work. As my acne started disappearing, I slowly came out of my shell, and I began making new friends within that group.

During my junior year of high school, I started to gain acceptance amongst the popular cliques of White Bear Lake High School. I got good grades that year and even made the varsity golf team, but as I got closer to all the cool kids, I noticed how my priorities were gradually shifting. I became more interested in hanging out with my new friends than I was in studying or sports.

As a result, I started to succumb to the typical peer pressure that permeates throughout every high school. I tried marijuana for the first time that year, got drunk, and started chewing tobacco. I started to do whatever the popular kids asked of me. I skipped classes, knocked books out of other kids' hands, and forged notes. I followed their mischievous acts just to fit in and gain favor.

Despite my experimentations with booze and pot, however, I finished with a B average, had a great golf year, and was an overall decent student. I hadn't been completely integrated with the cool crowd yet, so I managed to maintain my studies and conform to the school's curriculum. My only real downfall my junior year was getting caught using tobacco by my golf coach and losing my varsity letter.

That incident sparked my rebellious behavior as I entered summer break. I became closer with my new group of friends, older kids, and attended parties that I wouldn't have been invited to previously. I was drinking alcohol a lot more, smoking weed regularly, meeting girls, and coming home late at night—all to the chagrin of my father and mother, of course.

These shenanigans carried over into my senior year of high school. I was fully engaged in the social aspect of school but became disinterested in the whole educational portion of it. I skipped classes regularly and rarely did any of my schoolwork. If truancy and tardiness had been courses in school, I would have been given high marks.

I began to develop real friendships, though, and was attracted to the comradery and bond shared by all the people I was hanging out with. They all had each other's backs, and I wanted to show my loyalty and be part of that social hierarchy. I had missed that in the early years of high school, and now that I was finally a part of it, that's all I really focused on. Schoolwork and sports became an afterthought.

Not all of my friends were poor students. They already had the popularity, though, so they had time to concentrate on getting their homework assignments completed. I had to work on my popularity, so I put schoolwork on the back burner. When girls entered into the picture, studying became virtually nonexistent for me. Socializing became my number one priority.

As a result, my grades plummeted. I was getting Ds and Fs in most of my classes. I automatically made the varsity golf team my senior year, but as soon as the season started, my game suffered as much as my grades. Eventually, the coach told me I could no longer play on the team because of my failing academics, so I missed the rest of the season of golf.

I maintained a very lackadaisical attitude toward everything and was only interested in hanging out with my friends. I had so much fun with these guys that I didn't really care how my behavior was affecting my education. Missing only the popularity that comes with being a gifted athlete in high school sports, I was starting to find the recognition that I used to have in Texas. It was a great feeling to have, and that attention was guiding my actions.

I really felt fame and renown the day a group of cool kids approached me and asked me to partake in the greatest senior prank in the history of White Bear High. They told me how a few friends had been collecting money from fellow students for weeks so we could purchase a bunch of piglets to release in the school. The plan was to grease them up, paint numbers on them, and let them loose in the hallways during class.

All the logistics had already been worked out, they assured me, so all I had to do was help carry the piglets into the school and set them free. Not only did it sound fun and exciting, there was no way I was going to turn down being part of such a monumental event in our school's history. Besides, the prank sounded harmless—what could possibly go wrong?

The next day, a group of us met by the doors behind the cafeteria after lunch. Mark, Adam, and I waited anxiously for a U-Haul truck, driven by another student, to pull up next to the dumpsters to deliver the piglets. After what seemed like an eternity, we saw the lights and heard the beeping of a rather large moving truck backing up in the parking lot. Immediately, I started to wonder why they needed such a large truck for a half-dozen piglets.

The truck backed up and stopped, and a couple of students jumped out of the cab and came running toward the back door. Mark, Adam, and I ran out to meet them.

"Hurry, hurry—we've got to move!" they told us.

Adam unlatched the truck door, but the smell of shit and rotting eggs engulfed us all the instant he pushed it open.

"Oh, my God. What is that smell?" Adam exclaimed as he started to gag and dry heave.

Fighting through the stench, we all gathered our composure until we saw six large pigs covered in rotting vegetables and their own feces gathered in the back of the truck.

"Jesus, these aren't piglets," Mark complained nervously. "They're fucking sows!"

"Yeah, how the fuck are we supposed to get them inside the school?" I inquired. "They have to weigh fifty, sixty pounds!"

"We're going to put them in these gunnysacks and carry them," somebody yelled.

At that point, there was no turning back, so we all jumped inside the truck and attempted to herd the pigs into gunnysacks. The pigs squealed and squirmed their way out of our grasps. We fought feverishly with the large sows, slipping and falling on the fresh shit that coated the truck floor, and for a few long minutes, it seemed like we would never get these pigs out of the truck.

"This is pointless," Adam screamed, hurling insults at the uncooperative pigs.

"Guys, we need to work together," I instructed them. "All of us should go after one pig at a time."

"Yeah, be smarter than the pigs," suggested a classmate from outside the truck.

"Fuck you," Mark replied. "Get in here and help!"

After some tenacity, teamwork, and several minutes, we finally corralled the pigs and forced them into the gunnysacks. Sadly, they were too heavy to carry, so we had to drag them into the school one at a time. Once we got them through the doors, we pulled off the sacks and waited for them to run off wildly throughout the corridors of our high school. The pigs were terrified, though, and huddled together, frightened, in the entryway.

The prank was a spectacular failure. There were no greased-up piglets wreaking havoc and evading capture from teachers and staff, just a few scared pigs gathered together, waiting patiently for animal control to return them to the farm they were purchased from. Worse yet, word of the prank had spread like a plague, and school administrators had been anticipating our actions.

Adam, Mark, and I tried to return to our classes and inconspicuously blend right in, but we were covered in pig shit and the stench of a barnyard. As I casually walked into fifth period, my classmates all shook their heads and chuckled.

"You guys are so busted," some girl said to me, laughing aloud.

"What? Why?" I asked, attempting to mask my guilt with confusion.

A few minutes later, the teacher walked into the classroom and told me I was wanted in the principal's office. I stood up as my classmates cheered and applauded me for my efforts. As I was escorted through the hallways, numerous students patted me on the back and gave me high-fives. I knew I was in trouble, but I was relishing all the adoration.

Unfortunately, actions have consequences. Because of my failing grades, truancies, and multitude of absences, the principal informed me I was being expelled from school. He told me I couldn't attend the graduation ceremony, but I would still be allowed to attend the senior party at the end of the year. I figured I was going to receive the brunt of the punishment, so I tried to take responsibility for most of the prank.

In the end, I made a name for myself with my participation and exemplary leadership during our poorly executed yet brilliant school prank. It seemed to solidify my spot in the group of friends I so desperately yearned to be a part of. For me, the sacrifice was worth the reward. The popularity and acceptance were far more valuable than a high school diploma. Besides, I knew I could always just get my GED.

The worst part about not graduating was upsetting my mother. She didn't get to see my sister graduate because she dropped out of high school and ran away from home when she was sixteen. Now she wouldn't get to see her son receive a diploma either. My other sister had graduated, so I don't think my dad was as disappointed. My mom, though, had to be wondering where she went wrong, which is why my expulsion brought with it a small semblance of shame.

To make up for my failures that year, I obtained my GED immediately that summer, but I had no idea what I wanted to do with my life afterwards. I briefly contemplated joining the military or attending college, but only because that's typically what is expected from a kid once they're out of high school. Ultimately, I didn't want to leave my friends whom I was having so much fun with, nor did I want the burden of responsibility.

However, my parents made it clear that if I wanted to live under their roof, I needed to be working or going to school. I figured having spending money was better than homework and expectations, so I took a job working in a warehouse for a small ergonomics business. It was a mundane, nine-to-five job, but at least it got my parents off my back for the time being.

With a steady job and income, and a yearning for more independence, I sought to purchase my own vehicle. I was nineteen years old, though, and had no money saved or any credit established. I talked with my parents about possibly cosigning on a loan, but they were in the process of purchasing a new house and couldn't take on more credit. That's when my mom suggested I ask my godmother for help.

My godmother agreed to cosign on a small loan for me, and I purchased a bright red Honda CRX. I was ecstatic. It was a small, two-door hatchback sports car with a moon roof, and I couldn't have been more pleased. To me, it was the coolest car on the planet, and I drove around in that car like I was driving a Lamborghini.

I started to see my car as a reflection of myself, as strange as that sounds. Whenever I drove by girls or groups of people with my music bumping, everybody's heads would turn my way. Whenever I washed my car in the driveway, all the cute girls in the apartment complex across the street would sit on the stoop and stare. I loved all of the attention it brought me.

Once I got my own vehicle, it gave me a taste of freedom, and I started yearning for more. I also felt the pieces of a satisfying life coming together. I had great friendships, was attending fun parties, and was getting frequent attention from girls. Slowly, I was becoming aware of my potential, and I started applying myself more every day to become a better person—better-looking, that was.

CHAPTER TWO

◆ ◆ ◆ ◆ ◆ ◆ ◆ ◆ ◆

Something Special

EVEN THOUGH I HAD LOTS of friends, was dating frequently, and owned my own sports car, I still felt a little insecure. I didn't have the confidence that my other friends seemed to have and was somewhat shy at parties. Part of this was due to body image. I was very athletic and excelled at several different sports, but I was relatively thin, and people used to point it out. I was six feet tall but only weighed around 150 pounds, so I decided it was time for me to make a change.

I wanted to be bigger, more muscular, and felt it would give me the self-confidence that I was lacking. I had lifted weights in the past, but I rarely stuck with it for more than a few weeks. This time around, I was going to dedicate myself to lifting weights regularly, so I joined a local gym. The only problem was, I had no idea what I was doing.

I decided to hire a personal trainer, a kid named Tyler, so he could show me which exercises to do for specific muscles. Tyler was only a few years older than I was, but he was rather built and very enthusiastic. He taught me the basics of physiology and weightlifting, and my sessions with him were intense. He proved to be the motivating factor that I'd been searching for, and every day with him was an ass-kicking.

It wasn't long before I started to notice a difference. On my first day working out with Tyler, he took several body measurements. After thirty days, he measured again, and I was shocked at how much muscle I had gained. After my personal training sessions expired, Tyler encouraged me to stick with the program. He said that if I was still coming in six months later, he'd take measurements again. I had no intention of quitting and told Tyler I'd hold him to that.

For six months, I worked out religiously, always adhering to my schedule. If I missed a day, I was sure to make up for it early the next morning. I ate healthier, packed on the calories, and even started shaving my arms and chest to accentuate my muscles just like the bodybuilders did. I had more energy, never got sick, and was so much stronger physically.

One evening as I was doing a set of chest presses at the gym, I suddenly felt the weights get lighter as Tyler snuck up and began spotting me from behind.

"Five more!" he yelled. "Four, three—come on, Eric!"

I grimaced and struggled with the four forty-five-pound plates on each end of the heavy chrome bar as Tyler screamed expletives to motivate me.

"Two more, Eric—push! You got this shit!" Tyler prompted. "One more, one more!"

"Argh!" I screamed back as I pushed up the last rep.

Tyler cheered. "Great job, Eric. You're a fricking beast, bro."

I jumped up off the bench, gasping for air as Tyler gave me a high-five and handed me a towel to wipe the sweat dripping from my face.

"What's up, man? How you been?" Tyler asked excitedly with a big smile on his face.

"Good," I replied, still trying to catch my breath.

"You want to take some measurements before I head out?"

"Yeah. Let's do it."

The two of us made our way back to his office and engaged in small talk as he fiddled with his keys. Tyler acknowledged my consistent presence at the gym as he unlocked the door to his back office. He told me he was proud of me, informing me that most of his clients disappeared after a few months or only showed up sporadically. He was as encouraging as ever, and I could tell he took fitness seriously.

We walked into Tyler's office and he grabbed a tape measure and body-fat indicator, instructing me to remove my shoes and shirt. I slid off my Air Force Ones and took off my shirt while standing in front of the mirror. My tan body was covered in sweat, my veins popping and muscles bulging, still swollen from my intense workout.

"Holy shit, bro! You're ripped to shreds!" Tyler exclaimed, raising his hand up for a high-five.

I didn't even reply. Quite frankly, I was speechless. I simply stood in front of the mirror, flexing, with a shit-eating grin on my face. I'm guessing I had the same feeling as a metal fabricator or carpenter would have after constructing a fine piece of art. In fact, I felt like Michelangelo's statue of David. It sounds conceited, but months of hard work had completely transformed me. I was a new person, much to my betterment and delight.

I stepped on the scale and Tyler said, "Dude, you've gained eleven pounds! That's all muscle."

I smiled and flexed.

"You're at three percent body fat," he said as he pinched my skin with the metal device. "Damn, dude."

I just smiled and flexed again.

Tyler wrapped the tape measure around my body and referenced my file and early measurements. He went on to inform me that I had added considerable inches to my arms, chest, and back. I stood in the mirror and just kept smiling and flexing, and it was like I could literally see my body and ego growing in front of me, all in a very positive manner.

From that point on, getting ready in the morning or even going to the bathroom took longer because I spent so much time flexing in the mirror. Furthermore, what some might have mistaken for arrogance was just my confidence, which had increased dramatically along with my self-esteem. Going to the gym and working out became an addiction—the feeling it gave me was like a drug.

Now I felt I had the physique to go with my good looks—the missing link that really seemed to make my life complete both physically and mentally. I was no longer that tall, skinny kid who was timid, shy, and rarely approached girls. Now, when my friends and I went to parties, I always took the initiative when it came to meeting women. With my newfound confidence I was steadily becoming more of a leader, instead of the follower I previously felt relegated to.

I was still living at home, but with my own car and invigorated spirit, I was hardly ever there. I spent most of my time at the gym, with different girls, or partying with my friends. I always stayed the night at somebody else's house and was consistently late for work. Even though it was never more than five or ten minutes, my manager eventually lost patience with me and terminated my employment.

I didn't think losing my job was that big of a deal, but my parents made it clear I needed to have a job to remain in their house. After several intense arguments, I finally told my parents I was moving out. I packed all my clothes, put them in the trunk of my car, and just left. I didn't know where I was going—I just knew I didn't want to live with my parents any longer. I needed to spread my wings and leave the nest.

Not having anywhere else to go, I moved in with a girl I was dating who lived in West St. Paul. The two of us had been spending a lot of time together, so she invited me to stay with her until I figured things out. It was her parents' house, but her mom and stepdad were gone a lot and spent most of their time at their cabin in Wisconsin. If they were home, there was a basement door in the backyard that I could use to get in and out discreetly.

I also found a new part-time job working third shift for a small shipping company. It wasn't ideal, and I knew it was going to be temporary, but my co-workers were cool and smoked a lot of weed, so I lasted there longer than anticipated. I hated the work but there were no managers on the third shift and we goofed off a lot of the time, so it made the job at least somewhat tolerable and fun at times.

My living situation at my girlfriend's house wasn't optimal, either, and started to become more contentious once she discovered she was pregnant. Luckily, she and I agreed that neither one of us was ready to be a parent—otherwise, shit would have really hit the fan. The difficult decision was whether to choose adoption or abortion, which I completely left to her to decide. This was not because I was insensitive to either process but because it was her body, and I respected her choice.

To me, the situation was a problem, like the transmission in my car needing repairs. I preferred just going to the clinic and fixing the issue as soon as possible. That was my mentality at the time. I didn't even recognize or acknowledge the issue as a debate about life or death. I didn't watch or listen to the news. I wasn't religious, nor did I follow politics. My life was very positive, and I was only interested in having fun. That's all I cared about.

Once my girlfriend decided on abortion and went through with the procedure, it was like a huge weight lifted off our shoulders. The whole situation was stressful for me, so I couldn't imagine the agony it was causing her. I'm thankful we agreed on how to deal with the pregnancy because I wasn't ready to be a father. I had a couple of good friends who didn't get to have a say in the matter. They were going to be dads at an early age, and I didn't want that responsibility, not to mention the lack of personal freedom I'd have to sacrifice.

In fact, handling any major responsibility at this stage in my life was proving difficult as I began to experience the downfalls of trying to make it in the real world on my own. Car payments, insurance, filling the gas tank, even food was a struggle to obtain at times. After about two months of living secretly in my girlfriend's basement, it had become as bad as living with my parents. I finally decided it was time to go.

Unfortunately, my pride, reputation, and false bravado required me to move around. I refused to ask my parents for help. Sadly, I briefly felt like a loser, and that was a bitter pill to swallow. I sucked it up, though, and recognized my potential, so I reached out for support from family and friends and admitted I had reached a minor road block in my young life.

I called my sister on my dad's side, and she was sympathetic and took me in. She had purchased a home in West St. Paul with her husband, right down the street from my on-again, off-again girlfriend. She had two little kids and my newborn niece, though, and my social life soon clashed with her home life. We didn't fight, but we both felt the tension building. After a few months, we mutually agreed it wasn't an ideal living situation, and I had to move out.

Coincidently, my sister on my mom's side who had been living in Texas had moved back to Minnesota with her boyfriend and four kids around the same time. She had gotten pregnant at an early age and put herself through hell while living away from my mother and me. She wanted a change and to start anew, so she came back home. Her family was living in a duplex in North St. Paul, and she told me I could come live with her, so that's what I did.

At the same time, I also received a part-time job offer with a GNC (General Nutrition Center) located in a mall in West St. Paul. When I was living out there with my other sister, I had stopped in the store one day to get some protein powder and to put in an application. A couple weeks later, I had an interview but failed to follow up because of my living situation. This time around, though, I got the job. It didn't pay that well, but it was better than nothing. Besides, I got great discounts on supplements.

With a new job and a new place to live, my life finally had some stability. I may have been sleeping in the musty laundry room at my sister's duplex, but I didn't care. My clothes were all in a box, but I had complete freedom. My sister didn't care what I did, where I went, or when I came home. I always gave her some cash for letting me crash there, and my nieces and nephews adored me.

When I came home from the gym one day, my sister told me to go look at my two-year-old nephew. She pointed down the hallway toward the bathroom, and I went to see. There he was sitting on the toilet, looking at one of my body-building magazines—upside down.

"He's turning into you," my sister said. "Always on the crapper reading workout magazines." The two of us started laughing aloud.

The occupant in the duplex next to my sister's was also a single mom with four children. Whenever I came home from work or the gym, all the kids would come running up to my car to greet me.

"Uncle, uncle, throw me," they would beg excitedly.

They would all line up, and one by one, I would grab their arms, swing them back and forth, and toss them high into the air, catching them as they fell back to earth. My little nephew and neighbor trusted me so much I would actually flip them around high in the air several times like an acrobat. It drove the neighbor mom nuts, but the kids loved it. They'd laugh hysterically and demand I do it again.

Because I was only working around twenty hours a week, I had a lot of spare time for myself, which was great. I spent that summer lying out in the sun getting tan, playing with all the kids, and just hanging out with my friends and different girls. I felt like I was living a very fun-filled, stress-free, positive, and productive life. I didn't have a lot of money, but I didn't even care. The innocent laughter from all the kids around the duplexes was more valuable to me, as was my health, family, and friends.

CHAPTER THREE

◆ ◆ ◆ ◆ ◆ ◆ ◆ ◆ ◆

Introduction of a Lifetime

WITH MY LIFE HEADING IN a more positive direction, I figured it would be a good time to start looking for a new job. Even though I enjoyed working at GNC and was getting a great discount on all my supplements, it was still only part-time work and didn't pay that much. Then, while I was at work one evening, some masked men robbed a jewelry store a couple doors down from me, and that pretty much sealed the deal.

I started looking for new work and was lucky to be hired by a large and successful insurance company in downtown St. Paul. It was only a part-time position in the mail department, but it paid well, and my co-workers all seemed really easygoing. My work hours were from 6:00 a.m. to 1:00 p.m., so I had my afternoons free, which was nice. The only downside was getting up so early, but I was rather disciplined at that point.

Working in the corporate environment was so much simpler and easier than working in my previous employers' warehouses. It was clean and temperature-controlled, there were beautiful women everywhere, and we had a cafeteria with delicious food. I also was getting along great with everybody employed there. The department I worked in had a very laid-back atmosphere, and I absolutely loved going to work every day.

Because it was such a large company, there were numerous divisions within our building. A good portion of the mail, however, was only addressed to our company and gave no specific department number. Part of my job entailed opening the mail, reading the contents, and determining which department it was intended for.

One morning, I opened a package with just the company's address on it, and inside was a large package of mysterious white powder. The bag was stapled to a form that had the names of various chemicals listed on it. I looked over to my co-worker and asked her what I should do with it. She had been in the mail department for years and knew where to send everything.

"Dump it out on the desk," she joked. "Let's snort it!"

I had never done cocaine before, but the impression I got from my co-worker when we conversed was that she had experimented with drugs a little when she was younger. I took the package over to her desk so she could examine it more thoroughly. She looked over the bag and paperwork and was just as perplexed as I was, so she told me to send it up to the medical department.

The company did a lot of business in life insurance and had to review death certificates and other related medical documents. Because of that, we had our own medical department and doctors. With no other reasonable location for a bag of white powder and a list of chemicals, we decided that was the most logical place to send the envelope.

Later that afternoon, one of the vice presidents came down to our department and asked to speak with me in private. He was a cool guy who would stop down in the mail room from time to time and chat with us. Even though he was high up in the company, he was still very down-to-earth, so I didn't think too much about his request.

As the two of us started walking down the hallway, he asked me, "Eric, do you smoke?" He pinched his two fingers together, putting them up to his mouth as if he were smoking a joint.

I was a little hesitant to answer but reluctantly replied, "Yeah, I smoke once in a while."

I thought maybe he was going to ask me if I could score him a bag of weed or offer me some—I really wasn't sure. All I knew was that I was growing increasingly uncomfortable with the conversation and had no idea where it was headed.

We kept walking, and the VP proceeded to tell me about his friend in Texas who had mailed a package to him at work but hadn't put anybody's name on it. I was still thinking about marijuana, but as he kept explaining, I could tell he was talking about something else entirely. Then it hit me—the big bag of white powder!

"Are you talking about cocaine?" I asked.

Instantly, his eyes got big, and he looked at me with the most serious and concerned expression on his face. "Yes! Have you seen it?" he asked, disconcerted.

"Yeah, it came through this morning," I replied. "We didn't know what do with it, so we sent it up to the medical department."

"Will you go get it?" he politely asked.

There were a dozen things running through my mind at that point. I wanted to help the guy out, but not at the expense of my job—or worse yet, at the risk of going to jail. That was a lot of cocaine, and I wasn't quite sure I wanted to be handling it any more than I already had. Ultimately, I told him I wouldn't go get it myself, but I would call up to the department and inquire about it.

I ran back to my desk and called up to the medical department while the VP waited by the stairwell. I made up a story about a vendor sending a package of cleaning chemicals to the wrong address and described the package in detail. I asked if it was up there still, and the lady put me on hold while she checked. After a couple of minutes, she informed me it was still sitting in the mail cart.

That department was busy as hell, so I really wasn't worried they would be too interested in the package. Besides, who would even think it was a big bag of cocaine? I told the VP that it was still up there in the mail cart and that nobody suspected a thing.

He let out a big sigh of relief and thanked me repeatedly before quickly and discreetly walking toward the elevators. I went back to my desk and finished my day, but all I could think about were the crazy events that had transpired.

Shortly before my shift ended, the VP came back down to my desk and handed me an envelope. He didn't say a word—just gave me a shit-eating grin and a wink, and briskly walked away. At first, I thought it was money, a reward for my discretion, but then I realized there was no cash in there. I carefully opened the envelope, looked inside, and saw a bunch of white powder.

I was nervous and giddy just thinking about what I was going to do with it. I had witnessed people doing cocaine at parties before, and I knew some of my friends had tried it, but I had never done it personally. It had never really been offered to me, though, and now I had a bunch of my own. Should I sell it and make a quick buck, or should I try it? The possibilities were endless.

When I got home from work, I ran inside and called my best friend, Billy. Billy and I were as thick as thieves. We had become best friends toward the end of high school and spent a lot of time hanging out. We did everything together, so it was only natural we try cocaine together as well. I told him the crazy story about how I had obtained the drugs and asked if he wanted to try cocaine with me.

Billy enthusiastically said yes, so I rushed over to his house as soon as possible. I was still a little nervous and apprehensive as I arrived at his parents' place, but there was no turning back now. I rang the doorbell. When he answered the door, we immediately went upstairs to his room and locked ourselves in his bedroom. Billy pulled down a picture that was hanging on his wall and put it down flat on his bed.

"What's that for?" I asked, confused.

"Pour the shit out on this," he answered.

"Do you even know what you're doing?"

"Hell, yes!" Billy replied. "I've seen Scarface like ten times, bitch." We both chuckled.

I dumped the contents of the envelope on top of the picture as Billy started chopping up the cocaine with his driver's license. He then rolled up a dollar bill and snorted a big line like a professional addict. He handed me the rolled-up bill, and I snorted a line, too.

The drug seemed to have an almost instant effect on our personalities. I was overcome with adrenaline and a great sense of euphoria. Billy had a very boisterous personality and sense of humor, like a comedian, and he was always making people laugh. While we were in his room doing the coke, though, he became very timid and quiet as a mouse. Total buzzkill.

The drug had the complete opposite effect on me. I wanted to talk and have an engaging conversation about politics, sports, and even the universe. Normally I wouldn't even care about these issues enough to intensely converse about them with somebody, but while I was high, I was extremely motivated about everything going on in my life.

Billy just sat there listening, nodding his head, and chopping up the drugs. We listened to music, peered through his window blinds, and carefully watched out for his dad, who would be arriving home from work at any moment. Both of us were paranoid, oblivious to the side effects of the drug.

I left Billy's house late that night. As I drove home, I kept thinking what an awesome drug cocaine was. It was exhilarating, gave me lots of energy, and then just wore off—I felt completely normal again. It was the ultimate party drug, and I couldn't wait to try it again in a more social setting, especially with my friends who were already doing it. I saw the appeal of the drug and didn't really see any downside to it. Little did I know where my experimentation with cocaine would eventually lead.

CHAPTER FOUR

◆ ◆ ◆ ◆ ◆ ◆ ◆ ◆

Twenty-One Fun

A S THE SUMMER DREW TO an end and fall approached, several friends in our group started to turn twenty-one years old. These were mostly the older guys who had graduated a year or two ahead of us. Once fall arrived, a few more guys in our group had their twenty-first birthday induction into the official bar and club scene. The rest of us couldn't wait until our birthdays so we could join them all in the fun.

Fortunately, we didn't have to wait too long because one of our friends got a job working security for a nightclub in Minneapolis called Energy. It was an eighteen-plus club, so his job was to check IDs at the door and give wrist bracelets to those old enough to drink alcohol. Pretty soon, our entire circle of friends started hanging out there because he hooked us up with wristbands even though we were still under age. Best yet, it was a fun nightclub, and it quickly became our second home.

I loved the club scene because I enjoyed music and dancing so much—it didn't hurt that all the girls hung out there as well. Being able to drink while I was there just made it that much better. Some of us had gone to eighteen-plus clubs occasionally in the past, but this was a whole different environment of music, alcohol, and beautiful girls. I could easily spend all night drinking and dancing. It brought me so much happiness.

Ever since I was younger, I had always felt that I had another person, or maybe a spiritual being, inside me who loved to dance. I first felt it in fourth grade while breakdancing in San Diego Bay on a warm summer day. I thought that must be what they refer to as your soul. Regardless, every time good music started playing, something inside me just sprang to life, and there was no fighting it.

I would always put on music at home and dance in front of the mirror. I also danced while I drove in my car with the music turned up loud. Although I certainly didn't need alcohol to dance, it drowned out any fear or inhibition. I felt completely comfortable dancing alone, by myself in my own zone.

It also was a great body high on the dance floor with the bass pulsating through my bones. The club was more than just another bar to me—I connected to the energy, music, and dance floor on a much deeper level than any of my friends. Sometimes it was just me, the music, and some spirit-like dancing queen by my side, invisible to the masses of people surrounding me.

My friends and I celebrated New Year's Eve at Energy that year, and it was one of the greatest times of my life. The comradery between my friends, laughter, music, positivity, hordes of beautiful girls, and the jealousy from all the guys in the club toward my group. We were clearly the life of the party. We had no worries. Fun was our objective, everything came second, and we were all a big, happy family.

Better yet, I knew many more nights like that one were soon to follow. In eleven days, my twenty-first birthday would be upon me, and I was beyond ecstatic. This meant more clubs, more girls, more of everything. Excess wasn't a negative connotation at that time. From our perspective, there were zero ramifications from our shenanigans. My friends and I were invincible.

There would only be one other birthday to look forward to after that, and that would be my twenty-fifth birthday—the year the price of car insurance goes down. On your sixteenth birthday, you can get your driver's license. You can buy tobacco, gamble, and vote on your eighteenth, and your twenty-first birthday is legal fucking drinking age. Hallelujah!

There would be no more running from the cops and constantly looking over my shoulder. No more underage consumption tickets. No more hollering "Hey, you!" in the liquor store parking lot trying to get somebody to buy us beer. Freedom—that's what being twenty-one felt like . . . freedom! Even though I was able to drink at Energy I was still limited to that one bar. Now I could go to any club or bar I wanted to, anytime, anywhere.

The night of my birthday, I got off work and got in a quick workout because I knew I'd have zero motivation for the gym the next day. Then the plan was to change clothes and head over to my friend Jason's house in St. Paul to smoke a joint and have a few beers. After that, we were going to meet everybody at Waterworks Beach Club.

Waterworks was a bit of a dive bar right on the edge of a small lake. It pretty much looked like a large trailer home and was kind of dark and dingy inside. Better yet, we would go there when they had eighteen-plus night and always had a good time, and since my birthday fell on a weeknight, my friends decided Waterworks was the place to go.

Jason would drive, and I would leave my car at his house and spend the night. He had a house in St. Paul close to my work, so my plan was to sleep on his couch and go straight to work from there in the morning. I had forgotten to take the day after my birthday off work, so I figured this was the best way to maximize sleep and minimize my hangover. I'd heard what happened to friends on their twenty-first birthdays, so I knew what was in store for me.

After my workout, I arrived home to a pleasant surprise. When I went inside my sister's house, I was greeted by all the kids inside singing "Happy Birthday" to me. My sister baked me a birthday cake, fed me dinner, and made sure my belly was full and my liver was ready for the onslaught that ahead of me that night.

After showering, I found the perfect attire—my favorite black khakis to go with my new Doc Marten shoes which were trending at that time, plus a thin, long-sleeved sweater purposely too small to underscore my added physique. I further accessorized my outfit and adorned myself with some jewelry, combed my hair until each and every strand of it was perfectly in place, and then rushed to Jason's house, where he greeted me at his door with a fresh beer and a fat joint to smoke.

"Are you ready for this?" he asked with a sinister laugh and grin.

"Hell, yeah!" I replied determinedly. "I've been ready for this my whole life."

"I don't think you realize what's about to happen," Jason threatened jokingly as he took a big puff from the joint and passed it over to me.

Coincidentally, Jason had turned twenty-one only a few days earlier. He was also a Capricorn, and we had a lot in common—looks, personality, sense of humor, etc.—which is probably why we started hanging out frequently. He could attest firsthand to the liquid torture that I was about to be subjected to, and he kept giggling at my expense.

"You're about to be baptized in a river of booze," Jason warned me. "These guys show no mercy."

"How's this different from any other weekend?" I asked, annoyed.

"Because any other night you have a choice." Jason laughed. "Not tonight. You can't refuse birthday shots being bought for you. In fact, it's best you don't even ask what's in them."

That's when I became a tad concerned. I could binge drink with the best of them, but I typically stuck with beer. These older guys were much more experienced drinkers, some of them having gotten drunk as early as seventh grade. That night was like a rite of passage they had all experienced, and Jason was simply encouraging me to embrace it.

"Don't worry, buddy. It's going to be fun," he chuckled, patting me on the back. "Let's do a shot before we go."

As expected, the night turned into a complete shit show. My friends bombarded me with shots of alcohol one after another, like some sort of shock-and-awe campaign. It almost wasn't even fun as they kept trying to outdo each other in a sick game of who-can-come-up-with-the-worst-shot-for-Eric-to-consume. There was no getting out of it, either. With my group of friends, that's what occurred on your twenty-first birthday, like an initiation into a fraternity.

I tried to sneak off to the dance floor to avoid all the free drinks being sent my way, but eventually, some friend would always come to drag me back to the bar. I thought it would be so much fun turning twenty-one, but I believe it's more fun to watch your friend turn twenty-one and get wasted. The laughs from the peanut gallery grew louder with every shot I was forced to drink. The dance floor was no longer a refuge as I stumbled around to the music like a wounded animal.

Toward the end of the night, when I couldn't take anymore, my friends rested me against the wall on a bar stool. When I fell off, they jokingly handed me two pool cues to balance myself. They all chuckled as I tried to prop myself up only to snap both pool cues in half and fall to the ground. That's when the bouncer picked me off the floor and carried me to Jason's car. My birthday celebration was officially over with a fitting end to such a glorious and sacred tradition.

I woke up a little after 6:00 a.m. the next morning and felt like complete shit. It wasn't often that I got bad hangovers, but this morning was an exception. I felt like I had literally been hit by a truck. I still had on all my clothes from the night before, and as I stood in the mirror, I noticed I was covered in white dog hair from Jason's two massive St. Bernard dogs. My pants and shirt were wrinkled and marked with drink stains from the night before. I was a hot mess!

I hurried out the door and rushed to work as fast as I could. Luckily, my supervisor and co-workers knew it had been my twenty-first birthday the night before and showed me leniency when I finally showed up. I struggled through the first couple hours and was just going through the motions when my boss came up to me and told me I could go home early—a birthday present, he said. I was so thankful and relieved. His gesture further exemplified everything I loved about my job.

The birthday rituals continued throughout the winter and spring, and by summer, most of the guys were now twenty-one. We were all having so much fun together, too! I ran with a large circle of friends that felt more like a family. We laughed, joked, fought, and always had each others' backs like a close family would. We all had pagers and communicated with one another every single day. These guys weren't just my friends; they were more like brothers.

Nothing personified this brotherhood more than the night we all wore the same type of clothes to the club. I always wore tank tops or sleeveless shirts after I started working out, and one day, I decided to cut the sleeves off an old flannel I had in my closet. Soon after that, the look caught on, and all my friends started doing it—more so in a joking manner, though, not because it was fashionable.

One Saturday afternoon, Mike suggested we all cut the sleeves off flannel shirts and wear them out to Energy, which by then had changed its name to TNT. Of course, we all agreed, and more than twenty of us showed up to the club that night dawning sleeveless flannels. A sea of plaid blanketed the bar that night as we all walked around like alpha males on full display. We staked our claim to TNT that night—everyone knew the White Bear guys from that point on.

As a group, we did everything together. We hit up house parties near the U of M, and sometimes Somerset Camping Park in Wisconsin, right near the Minnesota-Wisconsin border. TNT became our spot, though, especially on Friday and Saturday nights. We could go to any other bar or club in the cities, but none of us really wanted to. TNT was so much fun, and because we knew so many people who worked there, we pretty much did what we wanted.

TNT was a huge nightclub and was always busy with lots of people, particularly good-looking women. The place had two stories, huge bars, and a giant dance floor. There were a lot of things about TNT that made it a great club and hangout, but to me, it was all about the music, dancing, and girls. Pretty much all the girls I was seeing at that stage in my life I was meeting at TNT, most of the time on the dance floor.

I became accustomed to dating plenty of pretty girls, but one night at TNT, I met one of the hottest girls I had ever laid eyes on. That night, my friends and I arrived a little early. We were just hanging at the bar when a group of attractive girls came into the club and caught my attention.

One girl with blonde hair in the group particularly stood out as one of the most beautiful girls I had ever seen. I was completely enamored with this girl and made it my mission of the night to meet her. My self-confidence was at an all-time high then—I felt there wasn't a girl out there I couldn't get, especially if she was on the dance floor.

I waited until later in the evening to make my move, after both of us had consumed a few drinks. I had never been intimidated by good-looking women, but this girl was different. This was the type of girl who gets hit on by guys all the time and has heard every cheesy pick-up line in the book. I really needed to be on top of my game if I was going to get her phone number before the end of the night. The stakes had been raised for me.

I watched this girl on the dance floor from afar. All the guys were gravitating toward her like sharks circling their prey, and she was rejecting every one of them. I could sense she was getting annoyed. This girl obviously had high expectations, standards I was certain I could meet. I just needed that perfect song to come on, and not just a song I liked, but one that I could tell she was into as well.

As soon as that track played, I slowly and methodically made my way through the crowd of people, moving to the music until I was right in her range of view. I watched for her eyes to look my way so I could gauge her interest. I wasn't going to push her like all the other amateurs in the club. This had to be a mutual seduction.

I danced right within her view, turning away several other girls drawn to the dance moves I was exhibiting underneath the flashing lights. I could tell she was starting to take a keen interest in me, and when our eyes finally met, she gave me a hint of a smile, exactly the sign I was waiting for.

I carefully and casually danced my way up next to her and asked, "What's your name?"

"Courtney," she replied.

"Hi, Courtney. My name is Eric. Do you mind if I dance with you?"

"Not at all," she said with a smile.

From that moment on, we danced the entire night together without ever leaving the dance floor. It wasn't just dancing, though—it was sensual and decadent, and we became lost in each other's eyes and in the music engulfing us both. I was captivated by her beauty. I tried not to stare excessively, but I couldn't take my eyes off her.

"I'm sure guys tell you how hot you are all the time, don't they?" I asked Courtney as we embraced one another, moving together with the music and energy.

"Yes." She sighed as if it were an annoyance.

"Well, that's because you're like a queen amongst peasants out here."

"My dad says I'm a princess."

"Queen, princess, angel . . . all of the above," I declared.

Courtney blushed and pulled me closer, and we danced together like we were the only two people in the club that night. I was completely oblivious to everything happening around us. It felt as if we had had a long and deep conversation without ever saying a word. I didn't know a thing about her, yet I felt as though I knew everything.

The music stopped abruptly as the lights came flashing on, completely ruining the vibe and pulling us back to reality. I took Courtney's hand and walked her to the door, shielding her from the hordes of drunken idiots trying to force their way to the exit. I waited by the entrance with her, holding her hand, never wanting to let it go.

"Can I see you again?" I requested. "Take you on a date or something?"

"Give me your hand," Courtney replied. She reached into her purse to grab a pen and wrote her phone number on my palm. "Call me," she said as she placed a soft kiss on my cheek and started to walk over to her friends.

I was watching her walk away in amazement, totally smitten, when she glanced back, whipped her long blonde hair to the side, and said, "You're a great dancer, by the way."

"Thank you," I happily replied.

"No, thank you," Courtney answered, smiling as she drifted away into the crowd of people leaving the club.

After that night, I couldn't take my mind off that girl. I called Courtney later in the week and asked her to dinner, and we started hanging out regularly. Dating her certainly wasn't easy, though. She was so hot that everywhere we went, she turned heads, drawing looks and stares from every guy who passed her way. Even other girls gawked at her. I used to enjoy getting attention but hanging with Courtney was like being stalked by predators.

When we went to different clubs and she would get up on the bar or stage to dance, guys would surround her, salivating at the mouth like a bunch of rabid hyenas. I had a lot of self-confidence and didn't really get jealous, but the type of attention she garnered would test anybody's patience. Sometimes I just wanted to punch in the face all the dudes who hit on her.

It was frustrating at times, but I always kept my cool. I looked at it as a compliment, and Courtney was always conscious of my feelings. She would come up to me when guys were all around her and grab my crotch. She'd start making out with me in front of everybody and tell me it didn't matter how many guys tried to talk to her, that she only wanted me. It made me like her that much more, and she liked that I wasn't jealous or possessive.

I'll never forget the night I made plans to meet Courtney and her friend so we could all go to TNT together. I went over to her house and waited as she and her friend got ready. Courtney's friend was a tall brunette with short hair, equally attractive. The two of them certainly weren't modest as they tried on different outfits together in front of me and asked my opinion as I lay on Courtney's bed, astonished by my good fortune.

The three of us drove to TNT together in Courtney's car. Right away, as soon as we had parked, security waved us to the front of the line. It was another perk that came with being around Courtney and her friends. They were so good-looking they always got preferential treatment whenever they went to nightclubs. I just smiled, enjoyed their company, and went along for the ride.

I went inside first and waited for them just inside the entrance as they got their wristbands. After a moment, Courtney came up to me and hooked her arm around mine as if I was going to escort her down an aisle. Her friend then came up to me on my other side. Much to my surprise, she hooked her arm around my left arm the same way.

The three of us strolled into the club together with locked arms. There I was with two of the hottest girls I'd ever seen on either side of me. As we walked into the packed nightclub, everybody was focused on me and the two stunningly gorgeous girls tightly holding me close as if I were their prized possession.

I tried to play it cool, but inside I was beaming with pride and glory. I was on top of the world right at that moment. Those girls by my side made me the envy of every guy in TNT and had every girl in the club wondering who I was. Furthermore, the looks on my friends' faces when I walked up to the bar where they stood watching us was priceless.

That moment truly epitomized my summer up to that point. All the hard work in the gym and at my job was paying dividends. The girls, all my friends, the comradery, the clubbing, etc.—I was having the time of my life and truly felt humbled by all the attention. I had worked so hard to achieve this level of happiness, and I wanted more than anything to keep the good times rolling.

CHAPTER FIVE

◆ ◆ ◆ ◆ ◆ ◆ ◆ ◆ ◆

On Cloud Nine

LIFE WAS TRULY AMAZING FOR me at that stage of my early adulthood, and things were about to get even better. My good friend, Jon, had a room in his house available to rent after his roommate moved out, and he asked me if I wanted to move in with him. He had a nice house in White Bear Lake where we always went after bar close to play foosball and continue our partying, so it would be a perfect living situation.

Things were going great at my sister's house, but it didn't change the fact I was living with six other people and sleeping in a dusty laundry room without much privacy. At Jon's house, I would have my own room, which was quite an upgrade from the laundry room in my sister's duplex. Besides, considering I spent so much time in White Bear already, it was a much more convenient location.

I told Jon yes without hesitation, and the following weekend, I packed all my clothes into a few boxes and moved out of my sister's house. Since I was moving into a new place, I figured I would get a new bed and purchased a nice futon for my bedroom which would give me a little bit more space. Jon helped me bring it in, and we set it against the wall in the basement with plans to move it upstairs later.

After I moved in, though, there was always something going on, and I never got around to setting up the futon or my bedroom. I always wound up sleeping on the couch in the basement. Jon and I joked about it frequently, always making plans to set up my room the next day or the following weekend, but then something would come up, or we'd be too hungover, and we would inevitably ignore it and put it off for another day.

I had a nice, new place to live in and was getting along great with my new roommate, but my expenses had increased considerably from when I was living at my sister's duplex. When a full-time position opened up in my department at work, I decided to apply for it because of the increased hours and significant pay raise. I was getting off work at 1:00 p.m., which was nice, but I had to be to work so early in the morning, and I really just wasn't a morning person.

This new position would be from 9:00 a.m. to 6:00 p.m., so I'd be getting an extra three hours of sleep in the morning, which was a huge incentive. I'd also get a big raise, which was important now that I was paying rent. More important, though, were the benefits, like health insurance and a 401k. I had never had health insurance, and even though I was young and healthy, I thought it was important at that stage in my life. Furthermore, I could start saving for retirement, something very few people get to do at such an early age.

After going through a few different interviews and anxiously waiting for a week to find out whether I got the job, I was called into my manager's office and offered the position. I was super excited, and the best part was being able to stay in the same department that I was already working in. I'd have the same manager and the same co-workers, which I was extremely grateful for because I was so close to everybody and considered them all to be good friends.

I couldn't have asked for a better summer at that point and was definitely riding a wave of good fortune as I lived the high life. I had a new job and a new place to live, and I was still dating Courtney, who was one of the hottest girls I had ever been with. I was extremely active—I was getting to the gym four days a week and still hitting up TNT every weekend, and Jon and I were always having people over to the house for parties.

I felt so energized and motivated that I even began to participate in activities I had given up after high school. Whether it was water skiing or swimming in White Bear Lake with friends, cliff diving along the St. Croix River, pick-up basketball games at the park, a couple different softball leagues, or something else entirely, I immersed myself in the outdoors. One sport I seriously started to engage in again was golf.

I really loved playing golf. There was just something so satisfying and special about crushing a drive three hundred yards down the middle of the fairway, and then making that long peaceful walk to the ball, surrounded by trees and the singing of birds along the way. I always felt so accomplished and elated. Furthermore, like all the other sports I was participating in, my golf game had improved dramatically because of how much I had been working out. I was shooting in the mid to low seventies on a consistent basis, which was not an easy feat.

After I turned twenty-one, the spring and summer seemed to fly by with how busy I kept myself, and fall was soon on the horizon. Things were going great with me and Courtney, but she started talking about moving to Florida to go to college. Despite all the great things I had going for me in Minnesota, I started to consider moving down there as well—not necessarily to be with her, but because of the warm weather and the chance to play golf year-round.

I was playing so well then, and enjoying golf so much, that I began to contemplate trying to play professionally. That summer, I was nearly a scratch golfer and was confident I had the skills to be able to contend with the pros. I was realistic, though, and knew I had a lot to learn before I could play at that level. That's why I considered moving to Florida and dedicating myself entirely to golf. I loved my job and friends, but the thought of the ocean, warmth, and daily golf was very enticing.

I always envisioned myself being the bad boy of golf, like what Dennis Rodman was to the NBA during that period. I would wear a sweater vest during matches, with no undershirt—just my arms showing with a bunch of tattoos, and a hat on backwards. It may sound corny, but I always thought professional golf needed somebody like that. It would have been great for the sport, and I thought I could fill that role perfectly.

Those dreams were short-lived, however, after Courtney and I had our first little fight. One night at TNT, I was dancing with a girl who wasn't twenty-one. I gave her a sip of my drink, so I ended up getting kicked out by security. All my friends were still inside, so the only thing I could do was sit in my car until bar close.

As I waited in my car in TNT's parking lot, Courtney found out what had happened and confronted me. We talked in my car for several minutes, and she asked me if I liked that girl. I told Courtney that no, I didn't, and that I was just being dumb, but I could sense she was still bothered by my actions. She had such a sweet, subtle demeanor about her—I swear she could talk the birds out of trees if she wanted, so I felt incredibly guilty over the incident.

After that night, Courtney and I didn't talk for a couple of weeks. The two of us weren't mutually exclusive, so I didn't think it was that big of a deal. I figured I'd just give it a few more days to let things blow over, and then I would reach back out to her. In the meantime, I continued enjoying all the good things I had going for me—sports, friends, family, partying, and living life to the fullest.

I was golfing with my dad at least a couple of days a week, playing softball with my friends and co-workers, and forming such tight bonds with everybody. I still dreamt of possibly playing golf professionally, but I had realized there was no way I could move to Florida and leave my friends and family behind. Besides, I had moved around enough when I was younger, and I had finally reached the pinnacle of acceptance and recognition that everybody seeks to achieve in life. Minnesota was my home, and I wasn't going any-where.

My first paycheck for my new position at work came the following Friday. Even with my first health insurance premium being deducted, it was the biggest paycheck I had ever received. I rushed to the bank after work to cash my check and then headed home to get ready for the weekend. I remember standing in the shower, reminiscing about the summer and all the blessings that had been bestowed upon me. I was singing, dancing, and smiling from ear to ear. I was so happy and content. Everything was perfect.

II

◆ ◆ ◆ ◆ ◆ ◆ ◆ ◆ ◆

THE DAY I DIED

CHAPTER SIX

◆ ◆ ◆ ◆ ◆ ◆ ◆ ◆ ◆

Manic Monday

AUGUST 26, 1996, STARTED LIKE any other normal Monday. It was a new week after another fun-filled weekend partying with friends, and I still felt enthusiastic about my new position at work. I wanted to go to the gym that morning because I had not worked out all weekend, but I had a softball game later that evening with my co-workers and I figured that would be enough exercise for the day.

It was a beautiful summer morning in Minnesota. I rolled down the windows in my car, put my Tupac CD in the stereo, and drove to work with the sun shining on me, happy as could be. Most people despised Mondays, but not me. Mondays were an opportunity for me to relay to my co-workers all the drunken adventures my friends and I had shared in the weekend before, and they always seemed to be entertained by my anecdotes.

Time passed as usual, and as the end of the workday approached, I told my co-workers I would see them at the softball game later that evening. First, I had to finish the rest of my shift, which usually didn't end until everybody else had left the office. As soon as the clock struck 6:00 p.m., I made my way outside to my car so I could rush home, change my clothes, and get to the park on time for the start of our game.

The softball league I was in with my co-workers was only supposed to be for fun, but we were all competitive and took it seriously. I loved playing with these people because not only was it a good time, the players were generally a bit older than I was, and I ran circles around them. I enjoyed watching the opposing team players back up all the way to the outfield fence when it was my turn to bat because I would hit a home run nearly every time I batted.

Summer was ending, and we were in playoff contention, so this game was a must-win situation. Because of that, I became extremely upset when I made a couple of costly errors that night, which was rather unorthodox for me. The problem was I was new to softball, and despite my tremendous athletic ability, I still had a lack of understanding of some of the fundamentals of the sport. I didn't cover the bases like I should have on a couple of plays, and as a result, we didn't get the outs our team needed to win. Ultimately, I felt my errors cost us the game.

Afterwards, I felt frustrated and agitated, so I convinced my co-workers to meet at a nearby bar for a few beers. They were unsure at first because it was Monday, but I persisted, and they eventually agreed. I was pissed that we had lost the game, but I was angrier at myself for playing like shit, so I needed a few drinks to relax. Together, a few of us split a pitcher of beer. My teammates weren't really in the mood to stay that long, but I decided to have a couple more shots before I left the bar.

As I drove back to my house, I felt a little buzzed and suddenly wasn't ready to end my night. It was only 10:30 p.m., and because I didn't have to be up so early in the morning for work, I felt I could still hang out a bit before I needed to go home. I decided to make my way to a friend's apartment to see what they were all up to and discovered everybody was partying over at Andy's house.

Andy was a good friend who lived in his parents' house, which was located across the street from White Bear Lake. We spent a lot of time hanging out there because it was a big house with a pool, a trampoline, and a huge backyard, and his parents were very hospitable. Andy's grandmother owned an even bigger house directly across the street from his parents' home, right on the lake. His grandmother had passed away a few months prior, so the house was vacant, and Andy would have people over there frequently.

By the time I arrived at Andy's grandmother's place, it was around 11:30 p.m., and I noticed several cars parked in the driveway and along the street. I made my way to the backyard and was instantly greeted with cheers and hugs from all my friends. I entered the lower level of the home and headed for the large bar that took up nearly an entire wall in the main room. Andy was behind the bar making drinks, and there were several half-empty liquor bottles and cups strewn across it, indicating to me the festivities had been going on for quite some time.

People were being loud, laughing hysterically, falling, and running around the house like little children. I could tell most of the people there were drunk already, and it was obvious I had some catching up to do. When Andy asked me if I wanted a beer or a drink, I immediately opted for the liquor so I could bridge the drunken gap that existed between me and everybody else at the party.

With my drink in hand, I ventured through the house and headed back outside to say hi to other friends. That's when I noticed some girls at the party whom I had never met before. One of my friends introduced me to them, and instantly, one of the girls became overly flirtatious with me. She was younger, I could tell, but still cute, so I flirted back. Flirting was all she was going to get from me that night, though—she was making her intentions abundantly clear, but my loyalty still resided with Courtney.

Eventually, we made our way back inside the house, headed over to the bar, and watched Andy as he lined up a bunch of shot glasses. He called everybody over, grabbed a bottle of Everclear from underneath the bar, and started filling the glasses. I wasn't excited about doing any more shots that night—not so much because I had to work in the morning, but because Everclear is a horrible tasting liquor and very strong. Everybody else was doing one, though, so I thought, When in Rome.

After a couple of shots, I was feeling rather drunk and had officially caught up with the rest of my friends. We were all having a ton of fun, so I kept on drinking. Somehow this night felt nothing like a Monday, and at that point I wasn't even thinking about work in the morning.

The music was playing loudly and everybody was dancing, when suddenly Andy came out into the living room dressed in an outfit from the 1970s. He looked like Jon Travolta from Saturday Night Fever, and everybody started laughing uncontrollably.

"Where did you get those clothes?" somebody yelled.

"Upstairs—there's a whole closetful," Andy responded with a laugh.

Feeling inspired and amused, a bunch of us made our way into the room where Andy had found the old clothes and immediately started raiding the closet. We all tried on different articles of clothing straight out of the disco era. Bell-bottom jeans, velvet blazers, satin trousers, platform shoes—the closet had everything. There were even afro wigs and feather boas that we used to accessorize our outfits.

The fashion show continued as we paraded throughout the house in our costumes, and the rest of our friends screamed and cheered us on. The scene was chaotic as we all danced around and fell to the floor, laughing so hard tears were streaming down our faces. It was immature fun, but I loved every minute of it. That's what made my life so amazing—innocent and stupid humor like that. It gave me such a great feeling, and by that point, I had completely forgotten about losing our softball game earlier that evening.

I finally settled down and helped Andy put the clothing back in the closet the best we could, and then I made my way back downstairs to grab another beer. The girl who had been following me around the whole night was still by my side. We sat at the bar as others went outside, just talking as I attempted to catch my breath and compose myself. It was hot in the house, and I was a little winded from all the pandemonium. That's when my friend came running in and demanded I come skinny-dipping with everybody.

I was hesitant at first but decided to follow my buddy out the patio door and into the backyard. The lake was just a few yards away and was separated from the yard by a four-foot-high retaining wall that wrapped around the property. There was a long deck that stretched out into the lake, but it was difficult to see anything at night. It was dark with nothing illuminating the water but the moon, but I could hear laughter and splashing from others who were already swimming.

It was early in the morning at that point, probably around 2:00 a.m., and a little chilly out. I was reluctant to get into the water at first, but after working up a sweat dancing in the warm house, I thought it might feel a bit refreshing. I walked up to the edge of the retaining wall with my friend and the girl and started to take off my clothes. I removed my shoes and socks first, then my shorts and tank top, but kept my boxers on because I still wasn't quite sure I wanted to swim.

I decided to test the temperature of the water first, so I sat on the edge of the retaining wall with my feet dangling just above the lake, and then hopped down into the water. I walked around a little trying to gauge the temperature, but the water barely came up to my ankles, and it was difficult to tell how cold it really was.

I climbed up the wall back onto the yard, took off my boxers, and stood there waiting for my friend to get in the water first. Out of the corner of my eye, I saw him jump into the lake feet first, so I immediately followed by diving off the retaining wall headfirst.

I had grown up with a pool and learned to swim at a young age, so I was a very experienced swimmer and was very comfortable diving into water. I was taught by both my sister and father to always put my arms in front of me to protect my head whenever I dove, and I remembered to do so even that night. In fact, that was the only thought in my head as I soared through the air—arms out, protect my head.

I hit the water, and immediately it was as if the earth ceased moving. Everything abruptly stopped and was eerily quiet. I tried to roll myself over and swim, but for some reason, I couldn't move. I tried again, but nothing happened. I didn't know why I lost all physical motor control—I felt completely normal, I just couldn't roll myself over for some reason. I kept trying to swim and turn onto my back, but still nothing happened. I just lay there like I was frozen in ice.

What the fuck was going on? Was I so inebriated that I couldn't even move? Was I dead? About a minute had passed by then, and despite being face-down in the lake, essentially drowning, I was confused and still wasn't all that concerned about my situation. I wasn't in any pain, and I knew all my friends were close by. Surely somebody would see me lying there and come help me.

I continued to try to roll myself over, but to no avail, and now I was gasping for air and sucking in water. A couple minutes had passed, and now panic was starting to set in. I opened my eyes in the water to see what was going on, but there was only blackness. I tried listening for my friends, but all I could hear were my own thoughts. My face was embedded in pebbles and sand, and I desperately kept trying to move so I could get air.

Why can't I move? Why can't I fucking move? I asked myself over and over. I felt myself start to drift away, as if my life was slowly exiting my body. Suddenly, I felt a hand on my face. I frantically bit the person's finger to let them know I was alive and that they should turn me over fast so I could get some desperately needed air to breathe.

All at once, I felt my face come up out of the lake, and I took a huge gasp of air. I was choking on water and tried to cough, but I couldn't even do that. I was breathing in air as hard as I could, and I could feel the life come rushing back into my body.

"What the hell are you doing, man?" I heard somebody say, giggling as if I were playing a prank on them.

"I don't know, dude," I frantically replied. "I can't fucking move."

I was still gasping for air but felt a tremendous sense of relief that somebody had finally turned me over. I could hear a female crying in the distance and the splashing sounds of others coming closer. I was looking up by that point, but I couldn't see anything. No stars in the sky, nobody's face—I could only see darkness.

"Hey, I need some help," I heard somebody yell. "Something is wrong with Anderson."

As I waited in darkness, I continued to hear voices, several voices, and then questions of concern. I could tell my friends were gathering around me, but I still couldn't see their faces.

"What's going on?" "What happened?" "Is he OK?" my friends were asking one another.

"Anderson, it's Shane," came one of the voices. "Tell me what happened, bro."

"I don't know, dude," I answered. "I dove in the water, and now I can't move."

"Can you feel me touching you here?"

"No!"

"What about here?" he asked again.

"No, dude," I replied.

"Do you have any tingling in your hands or feet?" Shane asked.

"Yeah, man, my legs are tingling," I said.

I felt two hands on both sides of my head, and then I heard my friend Shane say, "Nobody move him. Go call 9-1-1."

"Let's get him to the yard," I heard somebody else suggest.

"No. We can't fucking move him! Somebody go call 9-1-1," Shane implored.

Chaos ensued as everybody scrambled around the yard, knowing the police and paramedics would be arriving shortly. What started as a fun and lively party had now been turned into the scene of a tragic accident. I heard sirens in the distant and voices of the neighbors coming over to investigate the disturbance. I lay there in the water with my friends by my side and Shane holding my head.

I was slowly going into shock. I knew the yard was going to be crawling with police and strangers soon, and at that moment, I could think about only one thing. I wasn't concerned that I couldn't move my body or that I had almost drowned. I was only worried about the cold water's effect on my male appendage. Just like in an episode of Seinfeld I saw once, I was worried about shrinkage. I was afraid that everybody would see my shriveled up penis and think I had a small dick. Amusingly, that was literally my only concern at that moment.

"You guys, put some shorts on me," I insisted.

"What did you say, Anderson?" I heard somebody ask.

"Put some fucking shorts on me, please," I demanded. "Now!"

I wanted to make sure I was covered up before a horde of people and lights converged on the area. My friends scrambled to find a pair of shorts and put them on me as Shane held my head to keep me stabilized. I could sense the crowd around me getting larger and soon heard the sounds of CB radios crackling in and out. That's when I realized the police and paramedics had arrived, but everything was still black.

I was scared now. I didn't know what had happened to me. I didn't feel any pain, but I knew something was wrong because I still wasn't able to move. I heard more splashing in the water as people entered the lake and others moved out of their way. There were beams of light flashing around me, but everything else was still dark. I still couldn't see anybody's face.

As the paramedics approached, I could hear them asking questions as Shane explained the situation to them all. Shane was a certified EMT and was attending school to become a paramedic, and it was a blessing he was at the party that night. As they talked and assessed the situation, I started to fall deeper and deeper into my own thoughts. I was afraid and anxious, and I kept thinking about my mom. I just wished she was there with me so she could rub her hands over my forehead and tell me everything was going to be OK.

"Mr. Anderson, Mr. Anderson, can you hear me?" somebody asked.

"Yes," I replied.

"We're going to put this collar around your neck, OK? Then we'll put a board under you so we can carry you out."

"OK," I answered back with a whimper.

The paramedics worked to secure my head with a collar and strapped me to their trauma board while I listened to the sounds of people crying and panicking in the background. They lifted me onto the shore, strapped me to the stretcher, and then took me into the ambulance. I could hear my friends asking where they were taking me, and a couple of guys even tried to get into the ambulance to accompany me to the hospital.

"You can't come in here," I heard somebody say as the doors slammed shut.

During the ambulance ride to the hospital, I started going in and out of consciousness. I was still drunk, now in shock, and my body temperature slowly started to fall. We arrived at the emergency room, and I heard the doors of the ambulance being opened. The paramedics took me out and brought me through a large set of doors. Suddenly, everything became very bright. Even though there were numerous people surrounding me, I still couldn't see any faces.

I could hear the paramedics discussing my accident with the ER doctors and nurses, and there were specific terms about my condition that I keenly picked up: possible cervical fracture, spinal cord damage, no sensation, and paralysis from the neck down. I was no idiot. Despite everything that was happening to me, I came to the realization that I must have broken my neck, which was why I couldn't move.

"Mr. Anderson, we're going to take good care of you, OK?" I heard a doctor tell me. "You're in good hands now."

"Doctor, am I going to walk again?" I asked desperately. "Please tell me I'm going to walk again, doctor, please!"

"That's not important right now," the doctor replied. "We need to get some X-rays done first, OK?"

"Please fix me!" I begged him. "Please, doctor, fix me. I just want to walk again."

"Mr. Anderson, I need you to relax, OK?" the doctor said calmly. "Everything is going to be fine."

"I have insurance," I told him, as if that was going to help my situation somehow.

The concern and fear that consumed me just then were indescribable. As I was wheeled through the ER with the lights above whisking by, I just kept pleading with the doctor to tell me I was going to walk again, but nobody replied.

"Please make me walk again, please make me walk again, please . . ." I quietly whimpered as I slowly drifted off from consciousness.

While I was being prepared for imaging of my neck and spine, my body temperature dropped to 90 degrees, and I was now officially hypothermic. To raise my body temperature back up to normal, they wrapped me from head to toe in heating blankets with just my eyes and my mouth left uncovered. I was unconscious again for a short while as I was transported to various rooms throughout the hospital for X-rays and other imaging of my spine. At one point, I awoke while undergoing an MRI and briefly thought I was in a coffin.

After numerous attempts to get in touch with my parents, they finally arrived at the ER. The first person to greet them was the hospital's chaplain. Naturally, my mother assumed the worst. The chaplain took my parents into a separate room and told them that I was alive and stable but in serious condition. My mom didn't ask what had happened or what was wrong—she only asked to see me. The chaplain told her she couldn't right then, but he assured them a doctor would be in shortly to see them and explain everything.

He brought my parents into the waiting room, where several of my friends were waiting anxiously for some news on my status. The room reeked of alcohol, and my best friend Billy was sitting in a chair with his face buried in his hands, crying and distraught. Like a mother instinctively does, she consoled my friends, telling them everything would be fine. After about fifteen minutes, the doctor came in to update my parents and told them they could see me now if they wanted.

My parents were brought into the room where I was being monitored. As soon as I heard my mother's voice, I was instantly alert, and began to apologize to her over and over.

"Mom, I'm sorry," I told her. "I'm so sorry—I didn't mean to dive." I started to sob uncontrollably.

"Hush now," she replied. "Everything is going to be fine."

I'm not sure why I was apologizing—most likely for causing her distress and being a drunken fool. I just knew that I was sorry, sorry that all this had happened. I just wanted her to take away the fear and pain and make everything normal again.

My mother told me to be quiet and reaffirmed that she wasn't going anywhere, and I slowly drifted off into unconsciousness once again. Not too long after that, the doctors and nurses came into the room to get me and take me away to surgery.

I would spend the next several hours on the operating table as the skilled neurosurgeon put my neck back together and stabilized my spine. It would be another couple of days after that before I awoke again and had any sense or realization of what had happened to me.

I didn't know what my prognosis was or what the future would hold for me—I wasn't able to think that far ahead. Medically speaking I had no clue what the doctors could do to treat me. When I did regain consciousness, I just knew my life would never be the same again. I had a terrible hunch that the Eric I was before that fateful night was dead and gone forever.

CHAPTER SEVEN

◆ ◆ ◆ ◆ ◆ ◆ ◆ ◆ ◆

Born Again

SLOWLY, I CAME OUT OF a foggy haze and noticed a fluorescent ceiling light flickering on and off in rapid succession above me. I heard the sounds and beeps from various monitors, pumps, and other machines surrounding my bed. Instinctively, I tried to lift my arms to examine them, but I still couldn't move. Next, I tried to sit myself up, but that was pointless as well.

I attempted to move my legs, but they weren't responding to my demands either. All I could do was lift my head a little, until even that movement was impeded by a restrictive brace that was uncomfortably wrapped around my neck. If all that wasn't bad enough, it felt like a garden hose had been shoved up my nose and down my throat, and my mouth felt like it had been filled with sand.

Somewhere nearby I heard people crying and wailing, clearly upset and emotional. I heard others shouting and the sounds of a fist hitting metal or tin, obviously somebody taking out their anger and frustration on something. I remembered hearing that kind of commotion as I left Andy's house on a stretcher. I didn't like these sounds. I knew I was in the hospital, and clearly something terrible had happened to someone.

I didn't want to concentrate on what was happening near me or in the next room because I had my own problems to deal with. I wanted to know where my nurses and doctors were and why there was nobody next to my bed. I tried to yell for someone to come help me, but I couldn't even talk, not even a whimper. I couldn't push the call button or do anything but blink my eyes. I was alone and completely incapacitated, and I was scared. I was so fucking scared!

Sometime later, I woke up again. I wasn't exactly sure how long I'd been asleep, but at least now there were people and movement around me. The lights were on in my room, and nurses came and went from my bedside, changing IV bags and adjusting dials and knobs on the machines enclosing me. I tried asking one of the nurses a question, but no sound came from my mouth. I ended up just moving my lips back and forth, hoping she'd look down and notice me gesturing. I was desperate for somebody, anybody, to come tell me what was going on.

My legs burned like somebody had poured gasoline over them and lit a match. They also felt like they were bent up to my chest, as if somebody had been holding them there for days. I just wanted to straighten them out and stretch, but they weren't budging, and every effort I made to straighten them just intensified the burning.

I lifted my head and looked down at my body. My legs were actually straight out, so I couldn't understand why they still felt bent. I laid my head back down and tried to convince myself they were straight by envisioning it in my head. I hope this would make the burning and discomfort subside. My efforts were useless, though, and the feeling just wouldn't go away.

Finally, a nurse came to my bedside and said, "Hi, Eric, my name is Jill. Is there anything I can do for you?" She leaned in close, knowing I couldn't talk.

"My legs, they're burning," I mouthed, moving my lips as clearly as possible.

The nurse was apparently an expert at lip-reading and replied, "OK. Let me go tell the doctor, and we'll get you something for the pain."

The nurse came back a little later and explained that she was going to give me a shot of Demerol and would check back in a few hours to see how I was doing. She grabbed an IV bag and clipped it off at one end, injecting the Demerol into another part of the IV tube. It went directly into my vein, and instantly, a feeling of calm and warmth coursed through my body. It was a euphoric feeling, and I soon just lay there in that hospital bed completely unaware of anything going on around me. Eventually, I faded into a state of unconsciousness.

I awoke some time later with no sense of time or recollection of what day it was—it gave me an eerie feeling. Some nurse walked into my room again, and I was wondering if this was a new nurse, did a new shift occur? I started to try to piece together earlier events, attempting to form some type of timeline for myself. All kinds of thoughts and questions were racing through my mind as I desperately searched for answers.

The nurse asked me, "How are you feeling now? Are you still in pain?"

"My legs are still burning," I answered.

"On a scale of one to ten, what would you say your pain level is?" she asked.

"Eleven!"

"I'm sorry, Eric. I'm going to increase the dose of Demerol, and we'll see if that helps."

The next time I woke up, I saw my mom sitting next to my bed. I was immediately overcome with emotion. I would like to say I was happy to see her, which I was, but it was nearly impossible to experience any happiness in that condition. I definitely felt relief and comfort, though, and that was the first time I had felt either one of those emotions since waking up in the hospital.

My mom looked tired and stressed. I could tell by the look on her face that whatever I had been through over the last few days had been as hard on her as it had been on me. She rubbed my forehead and I told her I was thirsty. To my frustration, she told me that I couldn't have any water—I was only allowed chips of ice. She got up from the chair and told me she'd be right back, but I didn't want her to leave. Not for ice, not for water, not for anything. I never wanted her to leave my bedside again until I woke up from that horrible nightmare.

She returned to my room and sat down next to my bed with a Styrofoam cup in one hand and a little sponge and a plastic spoon in the other. She scooped some ice chips out of the cup and gently fed them to me, relieving the immense dryness I had in my mouth. She then lightly dabbed my lips with the wet sponge.

"More, please," I whispered as my mom fed me another spoonful of ice.

My mother explained to me that after the surgery on my neck, both of my lungs had collapsed, and chest tubes needed to be inserted to drain the fluid. When I was face down in the lake, I must have inhaled a lot of water. Since I was unable to breathe on my own, the doctors had to put me on a ventilator, and that's what I felt going down my throat. That's why I couldn't have any water, she said. She also told me that I had pneumonia and had to remain in the ICU until I could breathe on my own.

I wanted to know more about my condition, but it was just too difficult to ask questions or carry on a conversation. I knew things were bad—that was apparent—but I didn't know how bad. Usually, once somebody undergoes surgery for something, they get better afterwards, so that's the presumption I chose to go by for the time being. I assumed the doctors had fixed my neck, so once I cleared the pneumonia and started breathing again, I could be moved to physical therapy and resume my life. I realized it may have been wishful thinking, and I definitely was still worried, but I tried to remain hopeful because nobody had actually given me any prognosis up to that point.

My mom continued to feed me ice chips and told me about the friends who had already come down to the hospital to see me. She also said I would probably have more visitors later. My dad was working but would be down later that night, and my mom's boss had said it was fine for her to take some time off work to be with me throughout my recovery. She kept rubbing my head, doing and saying whatever she could to comfort her ailing son.

She told me about the family in the room next door whose son had tried to commit suicide by shooting himself in the head, and how he was still technically alive but on life support. His parents had decided to pull the plug and donate his organs, but were very tormented and upset by the decision. That explained all the commotion and crying I had heard when I woke up in the middle of the night.

Shortly after that, a young kid walked into the room wearing maroon scrubs, different from what all the nurses and personal care attendants (PCAs) were wearing. He was holding a black case, which he set down in order to pull out two paddles that looked like defibrillators. That's what I thought they were at first. I already had so many tubes and wires going in and out of me, and now I was thinking this kid had to restart my heart.

"Hi, Eric, my name is Chris," he said. "I'll be your respiratory therapist. How are you doing?"

"Terrible!" I whispered back.

"I'm sorry," he replied sincerely. "I can't imagine what you're going through. I'm here to help you get better though, OK?"

"OK," I answered back as the tears started flowing from my eyes. I was terrified thinking about what he was about to do to me.

"I'm going to press these paddles against your chest for a few minutes," Chris explained. "They vibrate rapidly to break up all the mucus in your lungs. Once I'm finished, I'm going to disconnect your ventilator and suck out all the mucus and fluid from your lungs. During this time, you won't be able to breathe. Understand?"

"Not really," I replied sadly.

Chris rolled me over a bit on my side and then began to massage my chest with the paddles. Pound. Pound. Pound. It felt like somebody was hitting me in the chest with a jackhammer! The pounding continued, and all I could do was lie there and take it. I couldn't moan, groan, or even put my arms up to block him—I just lay there helplessly while he pounded away.

The pounding continued for several minutes, and just when I thought I couldn't take any more, Chris turned off the machine. Instantly, I was overcome with relief.

"I'm going to unplug your ventilator now and insert this tube to suction out your lungs," Chris said to me. "You're going to lose oxygen for a minute, OK?"

"OK," I answered, as if I knew what was about to happen.

I watched Chris fiddle with the tubing until suddenly my oxygen was cut off, and I couldn't breathe. I was gasping for air and felt like a fish out of water. I tried flailing around, but I was completely helpless. Chris worked quickly to insert a tube, and that's when I heard a sucking sound—the sound one makes when they're drinking through a straw and finishing the last of the drink at the bottom of the cup.

I felt like I was drowning again, like the air and life were literally being sucked from my body. After a few moments, Chris pulled out the suction tube and reattached the ventilator, and instantly, oxygen came rushing back into my lungs. I took in a deep breath and then exhaled a sigh of relief.

That had been the worst feeling I had ever experienced. It was like I was being strangled to death and couldn't do anything to fight back. It was simply unimaginable—there's no other way to describe it. I was terrified, and I could tell by the look on Chris's and my mother's faces that they knew it. If I could cry, I would have been wailing, but instead, the tears from my eyes just soaked my pillow and sheets.

"Shh . . . it's done now," my mother said, trying to reassure me.

"I'm sorry, Eric. I know that sucked," Chris said to me sadly. "You're really sick, though, and we have to keep doing this to get you well again."

I understood he was simply doing his job, but to me, it was tantamount to torture. Pummeling my chest for ten minutes and then shutting off my oxygen, leaving me deprived of air and life—I just wanted him to get the fuck out of my room and never come back again!

After a few minutes, I calmed down and regained my composure, and that's when a nurse came in and told me I had visitors. My mom got up from my bedside to greet my friends and briefly explained to them my situation. She then brought them all into the room where they lined up against the back wall, waiting for the nurse to finish adjusting my bags and tubes.

As the nurse worked away, I raised my head slightly so I could see all my friends standing there looking at me as I lay in my bed. I may not have known before how dire a situation I was in, but by the looks on all my friends' faces, I surely knew it then. It was still summer, yet their faces were as white as the wall they were standing against. I could see it in their eyes and pale faces as they looked at me: complete fear, dismay, and sorrow.

56

It was obvious they weren't any more prepared for that moment than I was. It wasn't only my life that was turned upside down—my friends were experiencing the trauma of having to witness a brother cling to life in a hospital bed. They didn't know what to say or how to react. I could tell they all felt as helpless as I did as I lay there unable to move. Our summer was ruined, our lives shattered. We were still too immature and unaccustomed to process what had happened and what it all meant.

I felt their pain as I stared at the shock in their eyes and the blank stares on their faces. I wanted to cry more than anything, but I knew I had to be strong for all of us. I fought back the tears as they approached my bed and tried to make small talk.

"How are you doing, buddy?" Brian asked, trying to smile.

"You look great," Jon said jokingly.

Then my best friend, Billy, came up to me. I could tell he was trying not to cry, but he always wore his heart on his sleeve, and now he completely broke down. He bent down over my bed, burying his head into my legs as he grabbed the sheets and sobbed uncontrollably. My other friends tried to console him as my mom came back into the room to comfort him as well.

"I'm sorry, Anderson—I'm so fucking sorry," Billy wailed.

My other friends picked Billy up from my bed as they tried to hold back their own tears. Billy's apologies and grief set off an emotional chain reaction in the room, and the tears started to pour from my eyes as well as everybody else's. Even the nurse looked upset.

"Maybe that's enough for today," she advised.

"Yes, I think so," my mom agreed as she turned to the line of friends still waiting outside. "It might be best if you guys come back tomorrow."

It was an emotional ordeal. I was glad they came to visit, but the looks on their faces only reminded me of my grim situation. They all told me I was going to be OK, but they were horrible liars. After what Chris had put me through and the sheer agony I saw reflected in the pale faces of my friends, I knew my condition was not good. Whatever had happened to me at Andy's party that put me in the hospital was bad—real fucking bad, I thought.

Over the next few days, my condition worsened due to a bacterial infection that began to spread in my lungs. The respiratory therapists continued the pounding and suctioning while the doctors prescribed various IV antibiotics to kill the infection. The bacterium was a rare strain, and the doctors were having difficulty treating it, which complicated my breathing even more. My condition got so bad that the doctors were contemplating removing the ventilator and doing a tracheotomy.

My parents were starting to worry that I was going to die.

Fortunately for me, there was a highly renowned infectious disease doctor from Boston in town touring the hospital, and my doctors asked him to look at my chart and lab work. This doctor advised my physicians to use a specific concoction of antibiotics, and the infection in my lungs was brought under control.

As the week progressed, my situation improved dramatically. I was still undergoing the chest pounding and suctioning of my lungs, and I still hated every second of it. However, the doctors were secretly turning down my oxygen levels every day to slowly wean me off the ventilator. I figured out what they were doing, however, so I kept fighting with them to turn up my oxygen so I could breathe easier. But they wouldn't budge.

After I had spent over two weeks in the ICU on a ventilator fighting pneumonia and an infection, the doctors finally agreed to take me off the ventilator. That was such a relief. Now I'd be able to talk and communicate with people and, better yet, start eating and drinking like a normal human being. For the last two weeks, I had been fed through a tube and could only suck on ice chips to wet my dry mouth. I couldn't wait to finally drink a pop or juice—anything but ice!

When the nurse came into the room to remove the ventilator, I was thinking it was something I was going to be sedated or put under anesthesia for, but no such luck. She fiddled with a couple of clamps, disconnected a couple of hoses, and then slowly pulled from my nose a mucus- and snot-covered tube that was nearly two feet long. It was disgusting, but it felt so good to be free of that thing. It felt like a priest had just exorcised a demon from my body.

Now that I could speak, I had so many questions. For the last two weeks, all I had concentrated on was breathing and living. I was so sick and disoriented, I didn't even really contemplate my paralysis. I was in a tremendous amount of pain, and all the pain killers had left me dazed and confused. The situation was so surreal, I couldn't believe this was real life.

It was only a couple of weeks earlier when I had been on top of the world, living life on cloud nine. Everything had been so perfect, and suddenly I was in a hospital fighting for my life. How could something like that happen to me? That type of shit happened to other people—people that you hear about on the news. I couldn't truly accept my situation. All I wanted was for the doctors to tell me when I could resume my wonderful life.

CHAPTER EIGHT

◆ ◆ ◆ ◆ ◆ ◆ ◆ ◆ ◆

Prognosis

AFTER I COULD TALK AGAIN and the nurses could raise my bed to an upright position without causing me too much discomfort, the doctor came into my room one afternoon with both of my parents. He brought with him a large, laminated poster with a picture of the human body and central nervous system, like the ones hanging in a school's health class or a doctor's office. That's when he began a very detailed explanation of my condition and what exactly had happened to me.

Pointing at the poster, he showed me how my brain connected to my spinal cord and how my spinal cord ran down the length of my back to the crack of my ass. The doctor explained that the spinal cord was a bundle of nerves, kind of like an electrical cord, and that my brain sent signals down the cord to control all my bodily functions—like moving my arms and legs and going to the bathroom.

The doctor continued to point to the chart, detailing how the nerves branched out from every vertebra running down my spine into all my muscles and controlled function throughout my body. He then told me I had broken my fifth and sixth vertebrae in my neck when I hit the bottom of the lake. Those discs dug into my spinal cord, cutting off connection to the rest of my body. The surgeon had fused my spine together with a plate and screws, but now my spinal cord was trying to heal.

"There is a lot of inflammation around your spinal cord right now, Eric," the doctor informed me. "That's what's causing your paralysis."

"Well, am I going to walk again, Doc?" I asked anxiously.

"I don't know, Eric. It's still too early to tell."

"What does that mean?"

"You can still regain movement for up to two years after a spinal cord injury," the doctor replied.

"So I won't know if I'll walk again until two years from now?" I asked him impatiently.

"I'm not saying that. I'm saying right now it's too early to tell. You're still in spinal shock."

It sounded like he was beating around the bush, and I just wanted a straight answer. Was I going to walk again, or wasn't I? It seemed like a pretty simple question and answer to me. The doctor, however, emphasized that the central nervous system is far from simple—in fact, it's a very complicated organism.

"No spinal cord injury is ever the same, Eric," the doctor said. "The most important thing you can do is remain positive and work your butt off in physical therapy, OK?"

After the doctor left my room, tears flowed from my eyes despite my attempts not to cry. I was overcome with emotion and overwhelmed with information. It felt like I had just done eight years of med school in thirty minutes. My mom and dad did their best to comfort me, but I could see in their faces they were equally distressed.

My dad made comparisons to the situation he had been in when he dove into our pool while we were living in Texas. He had fractured two vertebrae in his neck and had to have a similar surgery to fuse his spine back together, but he had never lost any movement like I had. Between what the doctors were telling me, and what occurred with my father, I was only becoming more perplexed and frustrated with my prognosis and lack of clarity.

Over the next couple of days, I remained in the ICU while the doctors and nurses prepared for my transition to the rehab unit of the hospital. A physical therapist came in a few times a day and did range-of-motion exercises to keep my muscles stretched. Medical students and doctors in training would come in as well and poke and prod me, checking for movement and sensation. They continually asked me to grab their hand or wiggle my toes, always to no avail. I was terrified, unable to move anything below my neck, and felt extremely discouraged.

One night, though, as I lay in bed, I felt a glimmer of hope. My nose began to itch, and I wanted desperately to scratch it myself. I painstakingly tried to move my right arm up to my face, and slowly, I could see it responding—a few inches here, a few more inches there. Gradually, step by step, I worked my arm up to my chest, where I just let it rest for a few minutes so I could catch my breath. I could never in a million years have imagined that moving my arm would be so exhausting.

After a short rest, I decided to put every ounce of effort into my next move to get my arm up to my face and scratch the itch. I counted in my head—one, two, three—and flung my arm up into the air and smacked myself right in the face! It certainly wasn't graceful, and I didn't have much control, but I did it all my own, and I was proud.

Throughout the rest of that night, I continued to move my arms, alternating between the left and the right, moving inch by inch up to my face and then slowly back down to my sides. I was motivated and determined. This was how I was going to start my complete recovery and eventually walk out of that hospital to resume my perfect life. I was starting with my arms, and then I would move on to my legs, one painstaking inch at a time.

When the PT came the next morning, we capitalized on the progress I had made overnight, adding a little resistance training to strengthen my arms and improve control. It felt good to be working out and brought back memories of my time in the gym. For just a little while that morning, it gave me a small semblance of what it was like to be normal again.

My mom came by early that evening, and I showed her how much movement I had in my arms. She was ecstatic. It wasn't much, but it was a positive development—something to build upon and utilize to achieve my other goals. I conquered the infection and the pneumonia, got myself off the ventilator, and now had my arms moving again. I was feeling hopeful, and for the first time since entering the hospital, I felt happiness. I truly believed things were starting to improve.

A couple of days later, I was informed I was being transferred to the rehab unit on the sixth floor. With my things in tow, I was pushed in my hospital bed into an elevator, through the long hallways and into my new room. When I turned into my room, I was greeted by dozens of nurses and PCAs. Immediately, the nurses started grabbing all the tubes and wires, disconnecting them from one end and reconnecting them at another, and transferring everything over from the ICU bed to my new bed, which would be home until my recovery was complete.

At that point, another nurse marched into my room and said her name was Rita. She must have been in her mid-thirties, tan with blonde hair. She told me that she'd be my primary nurse while I was in the rehab unit and then immediately started barking orders at me about how I needed to be attentive and learn how to direct my cares, which meant I needed to start learning how to take control of my health issues on my own. With no pleasantries or empathy, Rita was strictly business, and to be honest, I was highly annoyed by her.

Once the nurses left the room, my mom came in. Right away, I started complaining to her about Rita.

"She's mean!" I exclaimed.

"She's just doing her job," my mom replied.

"Well, she could be a little more pleasant and caring."

My mom said she'd go pick up something for me for dinner and asked me if there was anything specific I wanted. For some reason, I was craving Kentucky Fried Chicken, so that's what I requested. As my mother left, another nurse came in, started changing out the IV bags, and checked my vitals, something they seem to do every fucking hour of the day while you're in the hospital. I noticed the rehab unit rooms had TVs, and I asked the nurse if she could set mine up so I could watch until my mom returned.

I had the nurse turn on the news so I could catch up on what was happening in the world since I had been absent from society for nearly three weeks by then. Most of the program was dedicated to the upcoming presidential election, with a brief weather forecast every few minutes. Fall had arrived, but the weather was still warm, and I just kept thinking how nice it would be to feel some fresh air on my face instead of the stale, dry air that permeated the hospital.

After the local news ended, an entertainment news program came on. The headline was the death of Tupac Shakur, a prominent rap artist who had been shot in Las Vegas a few days prior. I was in total shock. I loved music, especially hip-hop, and Tupac was my favorite artist at that time. In fact, his CD was still in my car stereo as I lay in the hospital. I watched as the host discussed his passing, and I just started to cry. His death was very upsetting and impacted me greatly.

My mom returned with the food, but I was too upset to eat. She asked me what was wrong, and I told her what I had just seen on the news. I explained to her that he was one of my favorite artists and that for some reason, I was very emotional about it. When I heard of Tupac's killing, it triggered memories of driving in my car with my windows down, playing his CD, singing, and just loving life.

His album had just been released in the spring of that year, and everybody was playing it at parties and in the clubs. I would rap along to all his songs every day on my way to work or the gym. I thought about dancing in TNT to his song "California Love" and wondered if I was ever going to be able to dance again. I loved to dance and couldn't even fathom never being able to dance in a club or with a girl like Courtney. After that, I just cried myself to sleep with my mother by my side.

I awoke early the next morning to my overhead light being switched on by a nurse who said he was there to draw my blood. Soon after, a PCA came in and started doing various chores around my room. After that came another nurse, a doctor, a horde of PAs, and a hospital administrator, not to mention patient after patient being rolled past my doorway. Unlike the eerie silence of the intensive care unit, the rehab unit was like a bustling downtown city on a busy Monday morning.

Eventually, my nurse Rita came storming in and opened the blinds, letting a flood of sunshine into my room. She started to write on the chalkboard a bunch of tasks and goals that were going to be required of me. I lay there and watched the list grow, getting more annoyed with every letter. Finally, she asked if I would like a warm shower, and I enthusiastically told her yes. This would be my first shower in weeks!

Rita wrapped a belt around my waist and lifted me from my bed into a shower chair. She then wheeled me to the bathroom and began to remove my stockings and hospital gown. For the first time since my accident, I saw my body in the full-length mirror that was in the bathroom, and I was utterly mortified. I couldn't even recognize the reflection in the mirror.

It took only three weeks to completely lose the muscle and physique that I had spent nearly two years working tirelessly to build and sculpt in the gym. I was skinny, my stomach was protruding, and all the body hair that I shaved off had grown back. My skin was dry and pale, and I looked completely emaciated. I remember thinking I looked like the Holocaust victims in the Nazi concentration camps that I had seen in pictures at school.

The paralysis that I was suffering from had totally decimated my entire body—I was so shocked that I couldn't even cry. I demanded Rita wheel me into the shower immediately. When I was finished, I closed my eyes as Rita dried me off so I couldn't see that zombie in the mirror. I had been completely oblivious to the transformation my body had undergone as I lay in the hospital bed for those first few weeks, but now the reality of my accident had completely set in.

After the shower, Rita transferred me back into my bed and put my leg stockings and hospital gown back on. She then told me I could start wearing clothes from home while I was in the rehab unit. That was welcome news because those gowns serve no useful function, and I knew that wearing regular clothing would return some sense of normalcy. I would welcome anything to help me forget about the ugliness that was hidden beneath the fabric.

As Rita finished, the doctor came in with his gang of physicians in training and began to poke and prod my body again. He tested my feeling and sensation, which were surprisingly substantial, as well as the movement in my arms and wrists. He told me the sensation and movement I had below my level of injury was encouraging and reminded me to keep working hard at my physical therapy.

He may as well have been talking to the wall, though, because my brain wasn't processing anything being said to me after that shower. His voice was nothing but background noise because I was so distraught at that moment. The image of my body was the only thing I could see, and my thoughts of despair were all I heard. I wanted nothing more than to curl up in a ball and die right there.

When the doctors left, Rita could tell I was still upset. She was a veteran nurse and had taken care of numerous patients with spinal cord injuries, so I'm sure she had seen every emotion the human mind could produce. Whatever the reason, at that moment, she instinctively knew exactly what to say.

"If you didn't like what you saw in the mirror, then you need to change it," she told me.

"How can I change what I can't control?" I barked back.

"Start with what you can control," she replied. "Worry about the rest later."

"I'm ugly!" I cried as tears streamed down my cheeks.

"No, you're not, Eric. You're one of the most handsome patients I've ever had." As she spoke, she gently put her warm hand against my face and wiped the tears from my eyes.

Until that moment I despised Rita's militant nursing style, but now I glanced up and gave her a hint of a smile, a silent thank you for making me feel good inside—even if it was only for a few seconds.

She smiled back. "Now go give those therapists hell today and show them what you're made of!"

CHAPTER NINE

◆ ◆ ◆ ◆ ◆ ◆ ◆ ◆ ◆

Let's Get Physical

LATER THAT MORNING, A YOUNG girl showed up to transport me to my first day of physical therapy. After a long journey through the hospital corridors, we entered a spacious, bright white room filled with assorted and unique gym equipment. There were large gymnastic mats throughout the room: cable and pulley machines, parallel bars, exercise bikes, and a bunch of weird games—basically a gym for a bunch of fucked-up people.

There was also a very diverse group of patients being treated in there as well, with all sorts of different ailments. There were patients who had strokes, people with brain injuries, burn victims, amputees, spinal cord injuries, etc. Anybody who required rehabilitation, as well as the numerous therapists helping them get back on their feet, could be seen scattered throughout the room. This was the part of the healing process most people don't ever see or think about, where the real work happens.

All these sick and disabled people once had a normal life just like me, and now they had to rebuild everything because it was shattered into a million pieces by a tragic event. Never in my perfect life had I even thought about all the hardships and suffering people endure every day, and there I was experiencing it firsthand along with them.

As bad as my situation was, I witnessed others in that room who were much worse off than I was. That's when I started to feel more sorry for them and less sorry for myself. It was definitely a reality check, one that proved just how much I had taken things for granted before my accident. I didn't necessarily feel better about my predicament, but it was changing my perspective on life.

As I sat there watching the other patients in the room, I could see the frustration and depression on their faces. A stroke patient struggled to hold himself up while trying to move his uncooperative legs. A therapist tossed a ball at a different patient sitting nearby, expecting him to catch it, but it only struck him in the head and knocked him on the floormat. Before my accident, I would have laughed at that shit, but now I only felt sorrow and pity—pity for me, pity for all of us.

Lost in my thoughts about the unfairness of life, I suddenly felt a tap on my shoulder. I turned and saw the same physical therapist who had been working with me up in ICU. Her name was Kelly, and she said she was going to be working with me while I was in rehab. She was nice, caring, and I was glad that I was going to continue to work with her.

She wheeled me over to one of the gym mats, sat down next to me, and began to go through the itinerary of what exercises we'd be doing during my stay in the rehab unit. As she discussed the reasoning behind certain exercises, she was impressed by my knowledge of resistance training and the different muscle groups.

"Wow, you know a lot about physiology," Kelly said.

"I was a gym rat before my accident," I replied. "I worked out a lot."

"Well, this should come easy to you, then!"

"It's not the same," I said despondently.

Kelly grabbed several large rubber bands, wrapped them around my hands, and tied the other ends to a door handle. She instructed me to pull here, push there, but I was unamused and bored. My muscles were weak, I had little function, and I couldn't stop watching the other patients in the bright room struggle like I was. Still, the therapists all remained steadfast and upbeat, encouraging every patient as if they were their last.

After my first PT session ended, I was brought back upstairs to my floor right in time for lunch, along with all the other patients in the rehab unit who were coming from their various therapy and rehabilitation sessions. I'd recognized most of their faces by then, but never met anyone of them personally, so Rita decided to start introducing everybody to me as if I was the new kid in class on my first day of school.

I first met a young kid named Chris who had rolled his car nine times and been ejected out the sunroof. He fractured a few vertebrae in his neck and had to wear a halo, a circular brace they drilled into his skull that completely immobilized his head. There was an older guy named Jim who had been in a workplace accident and was burned over ninety percent of his body. He was wrapped head to toe in bandages and looked like a mummy.

Next there was Melvin, a middle-aged, homeless black man who was robbed and beaten so badly it left him with a brain injury. Then I met James, a forty-something dad who had fallen off his ladder while working at home and fractured his neck, causing a spinal cord injury. James's injury was different from mine though—his paralysis was sporadic, affecting different parts of his body, as opposed to affecting everything below his level of injury like mine did.

After meeting the rest of the Addams Family characters who resided on my floor, I felt overwhelmed with emotion and compassion. It was a sober reminder of how quickly life can change for ordinary, average people just like me and the family members who cared for us all. Every night up until that point, I had cried myself to sleep asking "Why me?" but right then, I started asking, "Why us?"

After lunch, I was transported back to the physical therapy department to begin my occupational therapy. I was wheeled into another large, bright room that had mock kitchens and dining tables set up, along with a bunch of board games with LEGOs, wooden blocks, and toys you would find in a little kid's bedroom.

A woman who introduced herself as Jane approached me and informed me she was going to be my OT. Jane wheeled me over to a table and told me about what I'd be doing in OT. It was her job to help me overcome barriers and recover the skills that are essential for daily living.

"I understand you have use of your wrists?" Jane asked me.

"Yes," I replied. "Why does everybody keep bringing that up?"

Jane went on to detail the importance of wrist extensors and my tenodesis grasp. Moving your wrist in extension will cause the fingers to curl, or grip, when the wrist is extended. When the wrist is in flexion, the fingers will release, or straighten.

Jane instructed me to hold my arm out and just let my wrist go limp, and then lift my wrist up and watch my fingers naturally curl into almost a fist. She explained that this would allow me to grasp and pick up things without actually being able to move my fingers.

"You may not realize it now but having your wrist extensors is going to give you a lot of independence," Jane said. "That's why people keep bringing it up."

Jane got up from the table, and I just sat there letting my wrist go limp and then extending it back up, watching each time as my fingers naturally made a grip. I could definitely see what they were all talking about and why the doctors were so elated to see I still had that function.

Jane came back to the table with a box in her hand and pulled out the game Connect Four.

"Ever play this?" she asked.

"Yeah, when I was younger."

"Good." Jane dumped the checker pieces all over the table. "I'm black, you're red. I want you to pick up the chips using your tenodesis and put them in the slots."

I reached for one of the red chips, trying to place it between my thumb and index finger. I lifted my wrist to grab it, but all I seemed to be doing was pushing them around the table. I kept trying to lift the chips by extending my wrist almost like I was ice fishing and jigging my pole up and down. I finally got one of the chips between my fingers. Lifting my wrist, I grabbed the chip and ever so gently brought it over to the slot and released it.

"Nice work," Jane said as she picked up a black chip and slid it into the slot. "Now do it again."

"This is going to be the longest game of Connect Four ever," I told her, and we both chuckled.

For the next hour, we played Connect Four as I sat there trying to pick up the red chips piece after piece. It was very tedious and frustrating, but I never complained. I just continued to complete the task as instructed by Jane, trusting her expertise.

When our time ended, she told me I had an appointment with the psychologist whose office was just down the hall. I was exhausted at that point, mentally and physically, but apparently, this was part of my weekly routine. I used to spend hours in the gym lifting weights, running on a treadmill, or running up and down the basketball court. Now a simple game of Connect Four had completely wiped me out.

Jane wheeled me into the office and introduced me to Doctor Shevick. The doctor informed me she was the hospital's clinical psychologist, and it was her job to speak with patients such as myself who had experienced a traumatic accident and subsequent injury.

"So, how are you holding up?" Dr. Shevick asked.

"OK, I guess," I answered. "A little overwhelmed by everything, to be honest."

"Sure, sure—I bet you are," she answered.

Dr. Shevick told me that since I hit my head on the bottom of the lake, she wanted to conduct some tests to gauge my memory and cognitive abilities.

"Really?" I asked, annoyed by the thought of more tests. "I feel fine!"

"You hit your head pretty hard, Eric," Dr. Shevick informed me. "The doctors had to pick out little rocks from the lake bed that were embedded in your skull."

She grabbed a set of flash cards and told me to read the set of numbers on each card, memorize them, and then repeat them back to her. She held up the first card, which I thought was relatively easy. I looked at the first set of numbers, memorized them, and then repeated them back to her.

"3-11-18-5-9," I said.

Then the cards got gradually more difficult.

"7-2-12-17-9-2-4."

"Good. Now this one."

"5-9-11-13-3-18-22."

Then came a really large sequence of numbers on the next card.

"You can't be serious!" I exclaimed. "I couldn't fucking remember that before I hit my head."

"Good, that's what I wanted you to say," the doctor informed me. "You passed. Now, let's talk about your accident and how you're adjusting."

I told Dr. Shevick about my life before my injury and how happy I was—specifically about my body, working out, and being so active. I explained to her how I saw myself in the hospital mirror for the first time that morning and was devastated by the weight loss and transformation. I told her I was depressed and scared, and the tears began to pool in my eyes and stream down my cheeks. Despite all this, though, I did inform her I was more determined than ever to get back the body and muscle I had lost.

Dr. Shevick acknowledged my work ethic and motivation but cautioned me not to get too far ahead of myself. She started lecturing me on accepting my new body and moving forward. I didn't want to hear it, though. The doctors had told me I had two years to regain movement, and that was the prognosis I was going with.

"I'll never fucking accept this life!" I told her emphatically.

The doctor never responded to my comment. By the look on her face, I could tell she was surrendering our session for the day. There was no reasoning with me, not after everything I'd endured and all that I had lost. She could tell I was determined to return to my former life, even though she already knew it was an exercise in futility.

I got back into my room and asked my nurse to help me back into bed and turn on the TV. It had been a long and stressful day between PT and OT, not to mention the head games, and I still couldn't get that image of my scraggy body out of my head. Shortly thereafter, my father arrived at the hospital with some dinner.

He asked me about my day, and I told him everything—how I saw myself in the mirror and how the psychologist told me I should just accept the paralysis and my new body. I remember being extremely depressed at that moment. To me, physical and occupational therapy weren't opportunities for improved muscle movement and motor function. They were a harsh reminder of just how fucked I really was.

That's when I said to my father, "If I am going to be paralyzed forever, Dad, I don't want to live!" By that point, I was crying tears of fear and dread.

My father stood by my side and rubbed my leg. I don't think he even knew how to respond. He probably pondered my scenario and wondered if he'd want to live like that either. I don't think anybody really knows how they would feel, what they would do, until they're actually in that situation. I sure as hell didn't know. I was still trying to wrap my mind around how my life had suddenly landed me in a hospital rehab unit. The truth is, I don't even know if I meant what I said to my dad right then. I said it because that's what you're supposed to say in those situations.

"I could never live like that," people always say when discussing tragic events or traumatic injuries and diseases. It's almost cliché, a natural verbal reaction to an uncontrollable prognosis. I wasn't thinking that far ahead, though, and I certainly didn't have any suicidal tendencies. I think I was only repeating what I had heard in discussions and on television.

Over the next week or so, my daily routine was generally the same, but I could really start to tell my body was going through the spinal shock the doctors had warned me about. I was eating regular food and drinking normal fluids again, and now it was wreaking havoc on my bowel and bladder functions. I would wake up in the morning soaking wet from pissing myself during the night, or I would be sitting in my wheelchair and suddenly shit my pants.

This wasn't sporadic, either. I was either shitting or pissing myself on a daily basis.

Furthermore, I was having to learn ways to feed myself, dressing techniques, and other independent functions that little children are taught. I was a twenty-one-year-old guy trapped in a newborn baby's body. The night I dove into shallow water and broke my neck was the day Eric Anderson died, and waking up in the hospital was like being born again and starting anew.

These are not things teachers and parents prepare us for in life as we grow up. We go through life believing everything will be just fine. One day we'll get married, start a family, grow old, and eventually die. In between, we work, have fun, and pursue our constitutional right to happiness. Sure, there are some stumbling blocks along the way, but nothing of this magnitude.

I was not mentally prepared for the loss I had to endure then, loss that can literally drive a person insane. I almost believe there should be classes in school that warn you what it's like to battle paralysis, a brain injury, or something worse, like terminal cancer. Instead of bringing in some dipshit from D.A.R.E to tell students drugs are bad, they need to bring in a professional psychologist to inform kids about the absolute misery these diseases and injuries can have on you.

Knowing bad things can happen because we see it on TV or in the news is not enough—it just doesn't resonate or seem realistic. What happened to me and everybody in that hospital is as much a part of life as going to school or work, but most people are shielded from it, or purposely unmindful to the hardships that can be dealt to us anywhere, at any time.

I believe people want that shield, though, that false sense of security. Nobody thinks something bad like that can happen to them, but it can. I certainly never thought it could happen to me—never in a million years. Worse yet, I didn't know how to deal with the mental or physical aspect of paralysis. Not all the experts in every hospital throughout the world combined could prepare anybody for what I was experiencing at that moment.

CHAPTER TEN

◆ ◆ ◆ ◆ ◆ ◆ ◆ ◆ ◆

Leaving the Nest

WHATEVER DIGNITY I HAD COMING into the hospital was slowly being chipped away along with my masculinity and self-respect. Every time I shit myself, a nurse or PCA transferred me into my bed, removed my clothing, and rolled me over to wipe the excrement off my ass just like an infant. Getting catheterized by a nurse every six hours was no picnic either.

One night as I lay in bed trying to sleep, I experienced a very intense burning in my back and legs, probably the worse pain I had been in since being admitted to the hospital. I kept begging the nurses to give me something because the pain was so intense. After a little while, as I lay there in agony, I saw the door to my room open slightly. The light from the unit illuminated the first half of my floor and bed and standing in the doorway was an angel.

She wasn't a real angel, but the most beautiful nurse I had seen—if not one of the hottest girls I had ever laid eyes on. She had long, blonde hair and reminded me of Courtney. She must have been new, because it looked as if she was wearing a nurse's outfit resembling a Halloween costume as opposed to the scrubs nurses typically wear. I had never seen her before during my time in the rehab unit and briefly thought I was hallucinating.

"Hi, Eric, I understand you're in considerable pain," the nurse said to me.

"Yes," I replied, whimpering like a child.

"The doctor ordered an opium suppository. I have to insert it in your rectum."

I could only stare back, captivated by her beauty and completely emasculated and embarrassed.

Before my accident, this was the type of girl I picked up in the club. Now, however, I had been reduced to a weak, skinny, helpless cripple who was about to have a suppository shoved up my butt by a gorgeous nurse. It was official: the little dignity I was still managing to cling to was gone as soon as her finger went up my ass. I just wanted to crawl into a shell like a turtle and hide there forever.

The next morning, I still felt completely disconcerted by the humiliation I endured from having to deal with that beautiful nurse. I needed to know what my future was going to be like going forward. I was sick of the doctors always beating around the bush when it came to my prognosis, always giving me the two-year timeline bullshit. I wanted an answer finally.

I was waiting in my room for lunch one afternoon after PT when one of my doctors stopped in to visit. Dr. Shaw was one of my favorites—he was always so genuine and empathetic, so I decided to take that opportunity to try to get a straight answer from him regarding my paralysis. After some small talk, I said to him, "Dr. Shaw, will you answer a question for me? Honestly?"

"Sure, Eric," he replied. "What is it?"

"I want to know—am I ever going to walk again?"

There was a long pause as he just stood there staring down at me. It was obvious he was apprehensive about answering me, so I spoke up again.

"I know about the two-year window," I told him. "I'm sick of hearing that. You've treated dozens of spinal cord injuries. I know you know my prognosis! Just give it to me straight, doctor. Please!"

Dr. Shaw put his hand around the back of my head as if he was bracing me for something, and I could tell by the look in his eyes that he was bothered by my question. As he stood there with his hand on the back of my head, he looked right at me and said, "I'm sorry, Eric. No . . . you won't."

Hearing my doctor tell me I was never going to walk again was akin to him cutting open my chest and ripping out my heart. I was glad that he gave me a straight answer, but I was absolutely devastated by his response. I just sat there with a blank stare as the tears ran down my face. I tried to hold them back, but it was like somebody had opened the dam inside my head and the water came pouring out.

Dr. Shaw pulled my head in close to his body and kept telling me he was sorry as he tried to comfort me the best he could. I looked up at him with tears flowing from my eyes and thanked him for his honesty. He asked if I needed anything, and I respectfully requested to be alone. He patted me on my back, and I could tell he was at a loss for words.

After he left, I wheeled my chair over to my bed and locked the brakes, then put my face into the pillow and started sobbing uncontrollably. I had never cried so hard in my life. I was bawling and sniveling, pressing my face into the pillow as hard as I could so nobody could hear me.

Why, why, why? I cried and wailed. I was overcome with grief and emotion, and no matter how hard I tried to compose myself, I couldn't. I was truly heartbroken. I shouldn't have been surprised by Dr. Shaw's answer—the writing was on the wall—but I was.

Everything was still all very new to me. It had only been about five weeks since my accident, so I had just been going along with what the doctors had been telling me every morning, that it was still too soon to know my outcome. I just assumed that it was too early yet, and I was still within that two year window to start getting back function. Besides, I was regaining more feeling and sensation every day. I had even witnessed James across the hall moving his legs and standing up for short stints, so I was still hopeful that soon it'd be me.

That hope was now gone, along with everything that I cherished and enjoyed doing so much in life. I sat there crying, just thinking about golf, skiing, basketball, walking on the beach, feeling my feet in the grass, and dancing—I loved dancing so much. Now I'd never be able to do those things ever again. I didn't know if I could have children or even have sex. Even if I could, I'd never be able to play catch with my son or walk my daughter down the aisle at her wedding. All of that was gone, gone forever.

I completely lost my appetite after I heard the bad news, so I skipped my lunch. Instead, I stared blankly out the window. I remember it was a sunny day, and the heat coming through the window with the sunlight felt good on my face. Inside the hospital, though, it had never been so dark and gloomy. I wasn't very motivated for therapy after that conversation. I didn't feel much inclined to do anything.

Regardless of the bad news, I still had to go to my PT and OT sessions. The PCA came to my room shortly after and pushed me to the gym, where I just sat staring off into the distance as the tears slowly ran down my face. After a few minutes, Jane came walking into the room to greet me and quickly noticed me sitting there crying.

"What's wrong, Eric?" she asked worriedly.

"I'm just not having a very good day," I told her, crying.

Clearly concerned and upset, Jane looked into my eyes as I looked into hers, and the tears kept rolling down my cheeks.

"Would you like to talk to Dr. Shevick, the psychologist?" she asked.

"I guess so," I answered, although I knew there was nothing she could say that could cure what was ailing me.

Jane walked out of the room and returned a few minutes later to tell me Dr. Shevick would like to see me. She pushed me down the hallway to the doctor's office, and for the first time since we'd been working together, Jane left me with no words of encouragement. Only a gentle and noticeable sympathetic rub down my shoulder and back. A silent, yet emotional goodbye, knowing nothing she could say was going to make me feel better.

When I arrived at the psychologist's office, Dr. Shevick asked me what was wrong. I told her about my conversation with Dr. Shaw and that he had told me I was never going to walk again. She asked me what concerned me the most about that, and I started listing off the things I would never be able to do again. Over the course of the conversation, Dr. Shevick was attentive and tried her best to alleviate my concerns by telling me all the things I would be able to.

When I finished with Dr. Shevick and was brought back up to my room, I asked a nurse to help me into bed. I was emotionally drained and just wanted nothing more than to fall asleep and forget about everything I had been told that day.

My mom showed up a couple of hours later with dinner and asked me how my day went, and I told her the somber news that my paralysis was permanent. She didn't seem too surprised, though. She was older and wiser, and I think deep down in her heart she knew weeks ago that I wasn't going to get much better despite the two-year window the doctors kept telling us about. Still, it was a painful realization for my mother to accept, having to watch her child in so much agony and despair and knowing there was nothing she could do to help. All she could do was rub my head, wipe my tears, and cry herself.

I was crestfallen after Dr. Shaw confirmed my worst fear, and I started to basically just go through the motions during my therapy sessions. Every night I would cry myself to sleep; otherwise, I hid my true feelings from everybody, even my mother. It felt like the only remedy was to bury the pain deep inside myself.

Plus, I had so many visitors and so much support from friends, family, hospital staff, and even strangers. I didn't want them to see or know how sad I truly was on the inside. Nobody likes to be around Debbie Downer, I reasoned, and I knew I would need their continued support if I was going to get through my ordeal.

To her credit, Dr. Shevick did everything to help encourage me, including sending out a couple of mentors in wheelchairs to talk about living with a disability. The first guy just complained about doctors and insurance companies and ranted and raved about the politics surrounding the healthcare industry. I was terrified after he left and told Dr. Shevick I never wanted him to visit me again.

The second guy was a kid named Pete. He was a paraplegic, but he basically did everything an able-bodied person would do. He water skied and snow skied, played softball, rode a motorcycle, and more. Pete was what they referred to in the disability community as a supercrip. I started to feel inspired, but he was quick to warn me that as a quadriplegic, I wouldn't be able to do everything he did. However, Pete did give me some very helpful pointers about life in a wheelchair, and he encouraged me to keep living life and not to give up.

Pete told me I would need to buy my pants two inches longer so I wouldn't look like a dork waiting for a flood as I sat in my chair. He recommended sewing my pockets shut and stressed the importance of projecting a positive image in public. Pete told me to dress nice and carry myself with confidence. He also informed me of many negative stereotypes people in the public have regarding people with disabilities and how it was important for us to break those stereotypes.

Pete came to visit me a few times after that, and I felt more hopeful about my situation after our talks. He seemed to be living a rather normal life despite his disability, and he was truly happy. Watching and hearing about his life gave me inspiration that I could someday achieve that same level of contentment and optimism. Don't get me wrong, I was still rather morose about my predicament, but at least now there was some light at the end of the tunnel.

Over the next couple of weeks, my insurance company began to aggressively push the doctors to discharge me. I couldn't blame them—I'm sure I had racked up a sizable tab at that point. Unfortunately, I wasn't ready to leave the hospital yet. There were still too many unresolved matters regarding my care and living situation. Luckily for me, the hospital social worker was pushing back against the insurance company.

She was a big patient advocate and set up a meeting between her, my doctors, my parents, and representatives from the insurance company—a literal sit-down to discuss my fate. Thankfully, the social worker bought me some extra time, and the nurses and therapists started to organize a plan for my transition home. None of us could have imagined getting ready to leave the hospital would have been so chaotic and tiresome, but it was an exhaustive process.

The first order of business was getting a permanent wheelchair for me to use. The doctors and therapists advised and pressured me to get an electric wheelchair, but I refused. I thought an electric wheelchair would make me look more disabled, and I wanted a wheelchair like Pete's—one that looked cool and sporty. I was a quadriplegic, though, and the doctors and therapists didn't believe I could push around a manual wheelchair.

During our discussions regarding my chair, I expressed concern about public perception of me and my disability, as well as the fact that electric wheelchairs were so big and bulky. However, my therapists were still reluctant about the idea and doubted my determination. In the end, I proved them all wrong by independently pushing myself around the hospital in a demo chair provided by a mobility company.

With that issue settled, my therapists helped me get my own permanent wheelchair, and the nurses prepared me medically for my transition from the hospital. Rita had been on me from day one in the rehab unit about directing the people assisting me, and she continued to press upon me all the health risks I would face once I left the care of the hospital staff. I may have been coming up on my discharge, but I was still completely helpless and reliable on others for just about everything. It felt like information overload, so many things to remember, and I was petrified.

My whole life had changed dramatically, and I was only a shell of the person I had been before my accident. Paralysis, quadriplegia, wheelchair use, bowel programs, catheters, autonomic dysreflexia, muscle spasms, neurogenic pain, infections, pressure wounds, shifting my weight—I didn't know if I was going to remember all the proper protocols and procedures for dealing with all those issues.

The only world I knew while living with a disability was the world within the walls of Ramsey Hospital, and I had become cozy and content in that setting. It was stable, I always had a nurse or doctor to help me or answer questions, and the people I lived amongst were in a similar predicament. It had essentially become my safe space.

I didn't know what life would be for me like outside the walls of the hospital, but I knew I was going to be at a big disadvantage. As my new reality began setting in, I realized I didn't want to be discharged. I didn't want to leave my nurses and therapists, and I was nervous at the thought of not having a doctor at my beck and call. I was scared and cried tears of sheer terror, not knowing if I was going to survive without the support of the hospital staff.

In a way, I had been born again into a new life after my accident. The rehab unit was my home, the guys in the rooms next to me were my neighbors, and that was pretty much all I knew. I used to have the physical ability to overcome any obstacle thrown my way, but now I couldn't even push my wheelchair over an extension cord. I felt like a baby bird getting ready to leave its nest—without the ability to fly. Worse yet, I'd seen the nature channels. I knew what happened to those birds, and it usually didn't end well.

The night before my official discharge, I stayed up feeling nervous and anxious. Before my accident, I was always so happy and positive. I believed anxiety was a made-up condition, something inside people's heads. That whole night, however, I felt the full brunt of anxiety like a bunch of forty-five-pound dumbbells resting on my chest. I struggled to breathe. It felt like the entire world was ending.

In the morning, Rita came in and ripped open the blinds to my window as I shielded myself from the bright light like a vampire in the sun.

"Rise and shine!" she said enthusiastically. "Today is your big day."

"What's so big about it?" I replied.

"You get to go home. Aren't you excited?" Rita asked.

"Hardly." I answered despondently.

Rita started erasing all the notes, goals, and accomplishments written on the white board in my room—memories from the last month of my stay in the rehab unit. Throughout that morning, different doctors, nurses, PCAs, and therapists came to visit, say goodbye, and get me excited for my discharge, as if I were graduating college or getting paroled. Sadly, I didn't share their enthusiasm.

Going home was a bittersweet occasion. I had grown extremely close to my nurses and therapists. These people dedicated their lives to helping the sick and disabled, and they did their work with such empathy and care. They painstakingly nursed me back to health from the depths of hell that is a spinal cord injury, and I felt forever indebted to them.

Early that afternoon, my parents arrived and gathered all my belongings. Rita went over my discharge summary and meticulously reminded us all of what specific cares we needed to be especially attentive to. Listening to Rita read over everything, I felt like a ticking time bomb of medical issues. If somebody cut the wrong wire when I got home, BOOM!

After all the tearful goodbyes with hospital staff, I wheeled to the rooms of my fellow patients, people I had gotten to know intimately, so I could wish them all well. First was Melvin, because his room was right next to mine. When I peeked through the curtains, though, he was fast asleep, lying in a pile of cookie crumbs from the bag of chocolate chip cookies my mom had given him a couple of nights before.

I remember how content I felt with that last memory of Melvin. The poor guy was homeless, with no friends or family, but was so elated and grateful when my mother gave him that big bag of cookies. I wanted to wake him and say goodbye, but I knew what was waiting for him out in the world once he was released. I just wanted to remember him lying in cookie crumbs with chocolate on his face.

Next, I wanted to bid farewell to Jim, the burn victim, but he was getting his daily sponge bath, and nobody could go within ten feet of his room without a hazmat suit during that process. I felt so bad for that guy. He always said those sponge baths felt like being skinned alive. All I could do was tell the nurses I wished him well, and he would always be in my thoughts.

Chris and James, my other neighbors whom I got to know so well, had made significant strides in their recovery and had already been released several days prior to my discharge, so I said goodbye to some of the newbies in the rehab unit and the rest of the staff who had gotten to know me and my family so well. I then slowly made my way toward the hospital exit with tears in my eyes and a smile on my face.

As we drove away from the hospital, I kept thinking about the last time I was outside. I was partying and laughing with all my friends in the hot summer air at Andy's house. I stared blankly out the window, watching the world go by and knowing I would never be able to partake in it as I had before my accident. A couple of months back, I had the whole world right in the palm of my hand, and just like that, it was gone in an instant.

I leaned my head against the window as the tears ran down my face, doing my best to hide my sorrow from my parents. I knew my perfect life was gone forever, and as reality set in, the heartbreak and misery was almost too much for my soul to bear. No matter how much the hospital staff had done to prepare for me for life outside the hospital walls, I had no idea how I was going to make it in the real world as a quadriplegic.

III

◆ ◆ ◆ ◆ ◆ ◆ ◆ ◆

BACK UP ON THE HORSE

CHAPTER ELEVEN

◆ ◆ ◆ ◆ ◆ ◆ ◆ ◆ ◆

Homecoming

WE PULLED INTO THE ALLEY leading up to my parents' garage as my dad hit the garage door opener, revealing my Honda CRX parked inside. Upon seeing my prized possession, I was immediately overcome with emotion. I demanded my father close the garage door—I didn't want to see my car. My dad looked annoyed, but my mom understood, I could tell, and she pushed the button on the opener, closing the garage.

My car reminded me of my old life, my perfect life. I had so many different memories that involved my little Honda, whether it was driving to and from different parties and events with Tupac blaring out the speakers or sleeping in the passenger seat at Float Rite Park. That car was a symbol of the beloved life that I once had, and now that life was gone forever. As far as I was concerned, I never wanted to see my car again.

I transferred into my wheelchair, and my mother pushed me over the stone path leading to the stairs for the deck. A ramp had yet to be built, so the only way into the house was up the set of steps on our deck. The prospects of that feat were daunting. Disconcerted, I peered up the stairway to heaven, wondering how my parents were going to carry me up all those steps. I was terrified, but my dad assured me they had everything under control.

They tried to carry me up facing forward, but we instantly realized that approach put all the weight on the person in the back. My parents turned me around the other way, which we agreed was the safest technique. With my mom in the front holding my chair up, and my dad in the back grabbing the frame, my parents methodically bumped my wheelchair up each step until we finally reached the top. There was a little shouting and disagreement during the long haul, but eventually, the two of them got me onto the backyard deck.

We went inside the house, and my parents led me toward my bedroom, but as soon as I hit the carpet in the living area, I came to a complete stop. I tried to propel my wheelchair across the room, but it was like trying to push through sand. My mother got behind me to give me a boost, and I quickly realized how far I still had to go with my physical therapy. I thought I was making quick progress at the hospital, but that carpet was a reality check and a stark reminder of my limitations.

My mother unpacked my things while rambling off a long list of shit that still needed to get done. I had most everything I needed to live with my parents, but without a ramp outside, getting in and out of the house was going to be a huge obstacle. My father explained to me the issues with building the ramp, and all the codes and regulations making the construction a challenge. I was overwhelmed with everything at that stage, though, and just wanted nothing more than to relax now that I was finally home.

I went into the living room, and my parents helped transfer me into the recliner they had purchased for me. It felt nice to be able to sit on a piece of furniture for once instead of being in a hospital bed or wheelchair all the time. As I settled in, the phone started to ring as numerous friends phoned the house to check on my status.

One of the calls was from my old roommate, Jon. He informed me lots of girls were calling his house asking for me, and he just told them I wasn't living there anymore. Jon then told me Courtney had called numerous times. Knowing my fondness for her, he had decided to tell her about my accident. He said she was rather upset by the news and wanted to speak with me badly. I thanked him for letting me know and told him I'd talk to him soon.

After I hung up, I contemplated whether or not I should call Courtney. I didn't really care about the other girls—I knew who they were, but Courtney was different. She had cast some sort of spell on me the moment I saw her on the dance floor at TNT, and I still had strong feelings for her. I knew I had to talk with her no matter how hard hearing her sweet and subtle voice would be.

I knew it was going to be a very difficult conversation. Having just arrived home, I really didn't want to talk at that moment, but I didn't want to put it off either. I was very entranced by Courtney, and a part of me really missed hearing her voice. I thought it would be nice to speak with her after the last couple of months, but ultimately, I didn't know how either of us would react.

I sat on the recliner with the phone in my hand, just staring at the keypad and reciting Courtney's number in my head. I was extremely nervous and scared, and all sorts of different emotions were boiling over. After several minutes, I decided to just dial her number. I let the phone ring and ring until suddenly she picked up and said hello. Somewhat surprised she answered, I took a deep breath, tried to compose my emotions, and said, "Courtney, it's Eric."

"Oh, my God. What happened to you? Are you OK?" she started asking.

"Well, not really," I replied, not sure what to say to her.

She began to cry and told me that when Jon informed her about my accident, she didn't believe it was true. She even asked her mom about my injury because it all seemed so unbelievable. I understood what Courtney was saying—she wasn't being naïve. She was just shocked that something so catastrophic could happen to someone she knew and cared about. I still couldn't believe it myself. I tried to hold back my own tears, but they were impossible to control.

Courtney still really couldn't grasp the severity of my situation and kept asking me what was going to happen next, expecting me to tell her I would get better soon.

"I'm paralyzed, Courtney," I regretfully explained.

"Forever?" she asked, shocked.

"Yes," I replied, fighting back the tears.

"No, no, no! That's not true!" she cried back. "I want to come see you!"

"I'm not sure that's a good idea right now, Courtney."

"Well, when, then?" she asked desperately. "When can I come see you?"

I told her that I had just gotten out of the hospital and that once I got settled in, I would call her so she could come for a visit then. We cried together on the phone for a couple of minutes as she apologized to me for what had happened and told me how much she missed me. I thanked her for her concern and told her I missed her as well.

If she only knew how much I missed her, though—how much I missed everything. I missed her long blonde hair and her bright blue eyes. I missed the way she danced in the club and all the attention she garnered from everyone. I missed her smell, her soft skin, and her distinct perfume. I missed her laugh and her smile. More than anything, though, I missed the perfect life that she was a part of only a couple of months back.

I told her I would call her again soon, but that was the last time I ever talked to Courtney. I never wanted her to see me like that—ever! She was so beautiful, and I didn't feel worthy enough to be with her anymore. I had been reduced to a skinny, weak, helpless cripple who couldn't even go to the bathroom like a normal human being, very different from the handsome, athletic, and confident young man who made his way up to her on the TNT dance floor the night I got her phone number.

Courtney deserved so much better, I thought. Never in a million years would a girl that gorgeous want anything to do with a useless handicap like me. I was never going to talk to her or see her again; it would be too upsetting. I just wanted to forget about her and the person I was when I met her. That Eric was dead and gone, along with the perfect life I was living, and she was another chapter in my former life I wanted to close for good. I just couldn't take the pain.

I thought being at home would have lifted my spirits somewhat, but after my conversation with Courtney, I realized how difficult that was going to be. In the hospital, I was more or less shielded from the real world and real-world problems; now reality was thrust upon me. I underestimated how seeing my car would trigger memories of my past so quickly. I also hadn't anticipated how talking with Courtney would be so emotionally devastating.

I didn't feel like I was home; I felt like I was in a prison, both literally and figuratively speaking. First and foremost, it wasn't my choice to move back to my parents' house. Plus, with no ramp outside, I couldn't leave without being carried down the stairs. I couldn't transfer on my own either. I was virtually trapped inside that house in my paralyzed body—and worse, in my mind.

I went to bed that night haunted by my new surroundings. Before my accident, I would come home exhausted from an entire day of work and play and sleep like a little baby. That first night home, though, I stared up at the ceiling with the most dreadful thoughts racing through my head. When I got too uncomfortable or had to go to the bathroom, I had to shout for my mother. Yelling for Mom had become my new call button.

Before I knew it, the sun began to rise, and the light came creeping through the large patio door in my room. I spent that next day sitting in the recliner in my living room, watching television while my parents did various chores around the house. I was bored out of my mind and kept thinking about the different things I'd be doing if I didn't have my injury: working out at the gym, hanging with my friends, or getting ready to go to TNT to drink and dance.

It was a mundane existence to say the least. Not only did I have a spinal cord injury, I also had a severe case of FOMO (fear of missing out). My friends would call and check in to see how I was doing, but that almost made things worse. During small talk, they always had to mention what they had planned for the evening and then follow it up with a statement like, "We all wish you could join us!" or "Everyone misses you." I just wanted that first weekend to be over with as soon as possible.

The next Monday, my mom decided to go into work late so she could supervise the nurse and PCA that would be coming over. She wanted to make sure everything went smoothly and that they knew what they were doing when it came to my cares. The nurse and my mother tried to explain all my requirements to the PCA, and I could tell right away the girl was overwhelmed. She only lasted a week before she quit, so the agency had to find another PCA.

A week later, the nurse came to the house with a new PCA, a young kid named James. I wasn't comfortable with a male PCA. I figured if I was going to have somebody's fingers up my ass or grabbing my dick every day, I'd prefer it be the hands of a female instead of a guy. Beggars can't be choosers, though. If he was good at his job and dependable, then that was all that mattered. Besides, I had male nurses in the hospital, so I decided I would just do what I always did and block everything out while I was being probed and invaded.

Over the next week or so, I got to know James very well and learned he pretty much was raising his brothers and sisters on his own. His dad was one of the largest marijuana distributors in the Midwest and was serving a lengthy sentence in federal prison after getting caught with hundreds of pounds of weed. His mom was a crack addict and was always going in and out of jail and treatment.

James worked two jobs to make ends meet, and he even admitted to dealing drugs occasionally to pay bills. The kid wasn't bullshitting me, either. Not only did he look like he had had a rough childhood and upbringing, but the stories he would tell me about his dad and shit he'd been through were stuff somebody just couldn't make up. My days were filled with boredom, so I enjoyed listening to James talk about his life. I found him to be both amusing and fascinating.

James also had a rather volatile relationship with his girlfriend and was always asking me for advice. I was happy to oblige. If there was any subject I happened to be an expert in, it was girls. James would tell me stories about driving a truck full of weed up to North Dakota for his dad, and I would tell him stories about banging some chick in a Porta-Potty at Float Rite Park. We both found each other interesting in different ways.

Before James became my PCA, I was still waiting for the ramp to be built so I could start my physical therapy. I didn't really have any way out of the house other than getting carried up and down a flight of stairs. That was just too difficult, not to mention dangerous, but after James started working for me, he said that he would just carry me down the stairs himself. He was a rather big kid, so I told him if he didn't mind doing that, I would let him.

I signed up for services from a disability transportation company called Metro Mobility, and twice a week, I went to my physical and occupational therapy sessions. James would carry me down the stairs before he left in the afternoon, and my parents would lift me up the stairs when I returned in the early evening. That was my schedule for the next few weeks. Even though I was getting out of the house, I was still extremely bored and lonely.

One evening after I arrived home from therapy, I noticed a bunch of lumber and construction material stacked up in the backyard. When my parents came outside to help carry me up the stairs, they told me my cousins would be over that weekend to build the ramp. I was relieved. The ramp would give me a lot more freedom to come and go from the house, and I was hoping I wouldn't be stuck inside as much anymore.

I was happy a ramp was finally built, but it didn't do much to put me in the holiday spirit. Christmas and New Year's came and went that year without much fanfare or participation from me. I tried to put on a happy face for the family, but my mood was still rather glum, especially on New Year's Eve. I should have been at the club partying with my friends and dancing with girls. Instead, I was stuck in my recliner watching people celebrate on television.

A couple of weeks after that, my twenty-second birthday arrived. I wasn't feeling excited about that either. I remembered how much fun I had had on my twenty-first birthday a year earlier, and I knew nothing anybody could do could come close to replicating that occasion. I had friends call and inquire about my birthday plans, even offering to take me out, but my bowel and bladder issues still made my life too unpredictable for me to want to go out in public.

My plans were to stay at home and feel sorry for myself, which I had been doing a lot of that winter. However, my mother wasn't going to let me spend my birthday that way. She and my dad insisted that I at least go out to dinner with the two of them. It wasn't exactly an ideal scenario, but at least I would get out of the house for a little bit. They even said I could pick which restaurant I wanted to eat at.

My parents and I had a nice dinner together that evening, but I couldn't stop thinking about hanging with my friends the entire night. I was missing the comradery more than ever. I knew everybody was probably at TNT getting drunk and having a great time, and I wanted nothing more than to be with them all. That was the worst part of my accident and of being in a wheelchair—the feeling of exclusion I carried with me constantly.

When we arrived home after dinner, I wanted simply to go to bed and cry myself to sleep. My dad pushed me up the ramp while my mom ran ahead to unlock the door. Feeling dejected, I hung my head low as my dad pushed me into the kitchen. Once we got inside, though, my mom suddenly flicked on the light.

"SURPRISE!" A loud shout came from all my friends, who were gathered in the living room. I was completely shocked!

The inside of our home was decorated with balloons and streamers, there was a keg of beer in the kitchen, and our living room was packed with forty to fifty people. I was overcome with emotion. Instead of going to my room and crying myself to sleep, I now had tears of joy pouring down my face. The emptiness I had felt inside that whole day was now filled with the love and friendship from everybody in my house as we drank, laughed, danced, and reminisced.

I ran with a large circle of friends that summer, some I was closer with than others. There were certain friends who visited me frequently while I was in the hospital, and others I wondered why they didn't stop by very often. Everyone was there at my house that night, though, and friend after friend approached me one by one to apologize for not visiting me and to explain their reasoning.

Some hated hospitals, and others just couldn't bear the thought of seeing me paralyzed and a shell of my former self. Emotions ran high as we cried tears of grief, sorrow, and happiness. Ultimately, every single friend at my house reminded me they would always have my back no matter what, and we would get through the tough times together, like brothers and sisters.

When I was in the hospital, the nurses and therapists all warned me that my friends might not come around after my injury. That night, I knew that wasn't going to be the case with me. All the love I was shown that birthday evening proved my friends weren't going anywhere. My wheelchair didn't separate us after my accident—it brought us all together. Our bond was stronger than ever.

CHAPTER TWELVE

◆ ◆ ◆ ◆ ◆ ◆ ◆ ◆ ◆

Viva Las Vegas

SIX MONTHS AFTER BREAKING MY neck, it was time for a follow-up appointment with the surgeon who did my spinal fusion the morning after my accident. Doctor Gaines had seen me a couple of times after operating on me, but I was never conscious for those visits. I anxiously waited for that appointment to arrive because I had a lot of questions for him. Most importantly, though, I wanted to thank him for saving my life, because that's essentially what he did.

Dr. Gaines was a renowned neurosurgeon. During my hospital stay, nurses and other doctors frequently informed me how lucky I was to have him operate on me. It was hard to feel lucky in that scenario, but I understood what they meant. I was also told that Dr. Gaines was rather honest and blunt, attributes that seemed to be missing from all the doctors who constantly told me the two-year window bullshit when I asked about my prognosis.

When I wheeled into his office that afternoon pushing a manual wheelchair, the first thing he said to me was how surprised he was with the mobility that I had recovered.

"You were in pretty good shape when you had your accident," Dr. Gaines said.

"Yeah, I liked to work out a lot," I replied.

"Well, that's probably why you have as much function as you do. It might have saved you."

"A lot of people saved me that night, including you. I want to thank you for that."

"No thanks needed. That's my job."

After some small talk, Dr. Gaines tested my strength and sensation, and I asked him several questions related to my paralysis. Another reason I was anxious for that appointment was that I wanted to know about my future. I still had hope six months later that the wheelchair and paralysis weren't permanent, that science could one day fix my spine, and I knew Dr. Gaines would know before anybody. Furthermore, I was expecting him to tell me not to lose hope.

"Doctor, can I ask you a serious question?" I said to him sincerely.

"Sure, Eric. What is it?"

"Do you believe there will ever be a cure for spinal cord injuries?"

"No!" Dr. Gaines replied bluntly. "If there is, it will only be for acute injuries. There's still a lot you can do, so go live your life and move on from this."

I had just gotten a hefty dose of Dr. Gaines's bluntness the hospital staff always talked about. I didn't even know what the word "acute" meant then, but it obviously didn't apply to me. I was heartbroken. I wasn't sure why I was expecting a different answer—I just was. I figured that since science had accomplished so much by then, curing paralysis would surely be on the horizon someday. I guess I shouldn't have set myself up for disappointment, but all I was looking for was a sliver of hope.

I cried the whole way home from the doctor's office, and over the next week or so, I was rather depressed. I had already been told once I wasn't going to walk again, but I had never accepted that prognosis. How could I? How could anybody, for that matter? I was living in denial, I guess. It was all still too new at that time, and too much for me to wrap my head around.

It would have been easier to hear my function and mobility would improve someday—even if it would be twenty years later. However, Dr. Gaines told me the exact opposite, and just like my conversation with Dr. Shaw in the hospital, I wasn't mentally prepared for that response. His answer was like a punch to the stomach, and it upset me a great deal.

James, my PCA, could tell something was bothering me, so one morning, he suggested we take a trip. When I asked him what kind of trip, he proposed a road trip.

"Let's just get in my car and drive somewhere," he said.

"Where should we go?" I pondered aloud.

"I don't care," he replied. "Anywhere warm."

"How about a trip to Las Vegas?"

"Sounds good to me," James said, excited.

I told my mom what James and I had planned, and she wasn't exactly supportive of our intentions. She thought the physical aspect of being in a car that long would be hard on my body. I acknowledged the long trip may be a bit grueling, but I told her my depression was taking a toll on me. I desperately needed a change in scenery.

James and I planned to leave the following weekend. In the meantime, I needed to come up with some spending money. I was receiving Social Security Disability, but it was only $800 a month, and $600 of that I had to give to the state of Minnesota for my PCA services, so I wasn't exactly swimming in cash. There was only one thing I could do, and it was something I had been avoiding since I came home from the hospital—and that was to sell my car.

I loved that car but wasn't quite sure why I was still holding on to it. I couldn't stand looking at it because of the memories it brought back, but at the same time, I didn't want to let it go. I guess in the back of my mind I had this semblance of hope that I would one day get to drive it again, but Dr. Gaines pretty much ended that dream. I decided to put an ad in the classifieds and sold my CRX a couple days later, closing another chapter from my former life.

With some spending money in hand, James and I decided we'd leave for Vegas the following Thursday evening. Our plan was to drive straight through and arrive there exactly twenty-four hours later. James asked if it was OK for him to bring some speed for the drive there, and I told him it was fine with me. I had never done speed before, but I knew it was a stimulant of some sort, and I felt that we were going to need lots of stimulants for this road trip.

When the day came, we hit the road. After driving for about fourteen hours, we arrived in Denver, Colorado, where a massive snowstorm greeted us. The two of us weren't quite sure what to do, so we decided to pull into a gas station parking lot and do some drugs. James was getting tired from all the driving, and I was getting restless from sitting in the car for so long, so we decided a little pick-me-up was in order.

James chopped up a couple lines of speed for the two of us, and then we got back on the snow-covered road. After an hour or so of driving through the mountains and watching cars spin off the road in front of us, we started to regret our decision. Eventually, though, the snow abruptly stopped, and the sun shone bright in the sky. Just like that, it was a beautiful day, and James and I were relieved.

As we drove through Utah, I became enamored with the mountains and scenery and was glad we decided to make the trip. I could tell James was also glad as he gazed out his window in amazement. After a while, though, I started to get a little uncomfortable from sitting in the car for so long and kept thinking how nice a bed would feel. I was sure James felt the same way.

As we drove along the highway through the center of the vast desert, it was so incredibly dark that every star in the Milky Way seemed to light up the sky. When we finally approached the mountains, we couldn't help but notice how the sky in the distance had an awkward glow to it. Las Vegas wasn't yet visible, but the city's lights illuminated the sky above for miles, and I knew we were getting close.

"Why is the sky glowing like that?" James asked, bewildered.

"That's all the lights from the Vegas strip," I answered.

James glanced over at me with a big smile on his face as excitement and anticipation started to set in. As we drove through the mountains, all we could see was this massive array of lights in the middle of nowhere. The two of us were reinvigorated, knowing that we had finally made it. Viva Las Vegas!

I directed James to the Las Vegas strip, and we decided to stay in the Stardust Hotel. I told James that it was one of Vegas's first hotels and that one of his favorite movies, Casino, was based off it, so he was pretty excited. Furthermore, it was relatively cheap to stay there, so it would suit us just fine for our short duration in the city.

When we got up to our room, the first thing I did was call my mom and tell her we had arrived safely. She couldn't have been more relieved. James and I had been up for nearly twenty-six hours straight, and despite the drugs we had done on the way, both of us were exhausted at that point.

"Should we get some room service and then hit the hay?" James asked.

"Yeah, dude" I replied. "Steak and lobster sound good."

James called up room service, and it didn't take long for us to get our food.

As the two of us just sat in our beds eating surf and turf, he asked, "What should we do tomorrow, Eric?"

"Let's just walk down the strip and see what happens. Sound good?"

"That's cool with me."

The next morning, the two of us awoke around 10:00 a.m., and James helped me get ready for the day. We went downstairs, had some breakfast, and tried to come up with a plan for the day. James suggested we visit the Stratosphere Hotel, which was at the end of the strip and had a massively tall tower with a restaurant on top as well as a couple of rides.

The two of us had finished our breakfast and were sitting there relaxing, digesting our food, when I had an idea.

"I think I'm going to get a prostitute while I'm here," I told James.

"Seriously?" He laughed aloud.

"Yeah, why not? It's been nearly seven months since I had sex."

"Can you even have sex, if you don't mind me asking?'

"I'm not even sure," I confessed. "Maybe a professional can help me figure that out."

"Good point," James said. "Let me know how I can help." We both chuckled.

The two of us headed down the strip and attempted to go into several casinos, but James wasn't twenty-one years old yet, and he kept getting carded. That severely limited our Vegas experience, so we decided to go straight to the Stratosphere instead.

The Stratosphere Tower was nearly 1200 feet tall and had two rides. The first was a rollercoaster attached to the side of the building. The second was called the Big Shot, which shot you straight in the air at forty-five miles per hour and was the highest amusement ride in the world.

Once we arrived, we took the elevator to the very top and went outside, where all we could see was desert stretching for miles on end. That's when James suggested we go on the rides. I had serious reservations, but James tried his best to convince me. It wasn't so much that I was afraid of the rides—I just didn't want everybody staring at me as James lifted me in and out of my seat.

James kept telling me not to care what other people thought, and the more I pondered it, the more convinced I became. I was going to be in this wheelchair for the rest of my life, and I was going to be very miserable if I lived my life based off other people's perceptions.

"Fuck it! Let's do it," I said.

"That's the spirit!" James replied enthusiastically.

The young ride attendant who took everybody's tickets told me and James we could come to the front of the line. When it was our turn, James wheeled me over to the ride, locked my wheelchair brakes, and then picked me up in front of a crowd of people, placing me in the seat on the Big Shot. He sat down in the chair next to me while the other people in line got on next.

After a minute, a freckled-faced teenager came over and buckled my seatbelt, giving it a tug to make sure it was secure. When everybody was buckled in securely, the ride attendant let everybody just sit and stew for a while so the anticipation could build. As I sat in my seat nervously waiting, I look out into the crowd of people and saw every single person staring at me.

"Why is everybody staring at me, James?" I asked, disconcerted.

Suddenly, the ride shot us into the air at forty-five miles per hour. Because I was so skinny and couldn't hold onto the locking mechanism that fits over your shoulders, I fell straight down almost out of my seat, just hanging by the seat belt wrapped loosely around my waist. Everybody on the ride, including James, was peering out into the vast desert landscape from a thousand feet above sea level, but the horde of people below gawked at me as I barely clung to my chair. I even heard people screaming. I was in a complete state of panic and disbelief.

Before I could even process the severity of my situation, the ride slowly started to lower back to the roof. James finally looked over at me in shock, quickly grabbing my arms and attempting to pull me back up. I was literally clinging to the ride like a wet towel hung from a clothesline.

As the ride continued to lower, a group of guys came running over to prop me back up so my legs weren't crushed between the seat and ground. As I looked at the crowd, all I could see were people with their hands covering their mouths and complete terror in their eyes. As I finally got situated back up in my seat, a few more people came running over to help. The entire ordeal completely took my breath away. A few seconds of terror and I felt like I had run a marathon.

"My God, are you OK?" somebody asked.

"Yes, thank you," I gasped.

"I thought you were going to fall out of there!" another exclaimed.

"So did I," I answered anxiously.

James lifted me out of the seat and put me back in my wheelchair, giggling like a schoolgirl the whole time.

"What the fuck are you laughing about?" I asked James sternly.

"That was insane!" James answered, still chuckling.

"Yeah, you're telling me!" I replied. "I'm not going on that fucking rollercoaster!"

Everybody laughed aloud.

As we headed back to the entrance, the crowd moved out of my way. People started to come up to me to express their concern and relief, and I thanked them all for their kindness. At the door, we were met by a manager who started yelling at me for being on the ride. He pointed to a sign displayed at the front of the line which detailed various medical conditions that should exclude certain people from riding the Big Shot.

Apparently, when normal people go on rollercoasters and other rides, muscles throughout their bodies contract to fight the g-force they're being subjected to, keeping them securely in place. If somebody like me is paralyzed from the chest down with no use of their abdominal muscles, they're at the mercy of gravity and can be thrown around the ride and even ejected from their seat.

"Cut me some slack, man," I said to the manager. I explained that I had only been in a wheelchair for six months, and the ride attendant hadn't said shit to us.

"Yeah, fuck off," James barked, giving the guy the middle finger.

The two of us laughed as we headed back down to the restaurant to sit for a minute and gather our composure.

"Well, I guess I won't be going on any more amusement rides," I told James.

"What about Ferris wheels?" he replied.

"Screw you."

"Merry-go-rounds?"

"Haha, funny." The two of us giggled like children.

We headed back down to the strip and began our journey back to our hotel. I kept thinking about the harsh learning experience I had just endured. Obviously, there are some things the doctors and therapists simply can't prepare you for, and you're left to figure them out on your own—like gravity's effect on a paralyzed body.

James and I returned to our hotel room and cleaned up a little before dinner. We decided to go into downtown Vegas to eat so I could show James Fremont Street. Shortly before my accident, I traveled to Vegas with a group of co-workers, and we all stayed downtown, so I knew James would enjoy the light show and all the performers who dressed up and hung around there. We cruised around Fremont Street for a bit, taking pictures, and then had a nice steak dinner before heading back to our hotel.

After dinner, I reminded James of my decision to get a prostitute and asked if he'd mind if I had the room for a couple of hours. He was more than supportive and brought me back upstairs to help me prepare for my big date. I asked him to go to the cash machine for me, and then the two of us combed through the Vegas Yellow Pages looking for the perfect girl.

I called an agency to request a girl, and thirty minutes later, a female called our hotel phone and asked to be let up to our room. I sent James down to retrieve my escort while I smoked a little weed to help calm my nerves. I felt like I was in junior high getting ready to ask my school crush to a dance. I wasn't used to that type of discomfort. I had always been so confident and smooth when it came to picking up women, but now I was paralyzed and had no clue how to act or say in front of girls—even if they were escorts.

Finally, after what seemed like an eternity, a beautiful redhead entered my room and introduced herself. Right away, I just decided to be open and honest about my paralysis—I felt there was simply no other approach. And to my surprise, the lovely lady was not deterred one bit. From there, the negotiations began, as the escort gave me the price list in a rather upfront manner.

"It's $200 for a hand job, $400 for a blow job, and $600 for sex," she informed me.

"Well, I don't want a blow job, I can give myself a hand job, and I'm not sure I want to pay $600 for an act I'm not sure I'm even able to perform," I replied.

"OK. What would you like to do then, sweetie?"

I explained to the nice girl I only had $300 and would appreciate if she'd just help me explore my newfound sexuality. She took my cash, took off her clothes, and then started kissing me while grinding on my lap. She grabbed my crotch, and I was able to get an erection, so I was a little relieved about that. I buried my face in her voluptuous breasts, and I was definitely aroused, but quite frankly, I wanted to have sex.

Unfortunately, I didn't have three hundred more dollars. More importantly, I had no idea what I was doing. It was total fucking amateur hour in a hotel in Las Vegas with a gorgeous prostitute, and I lay there like I was twelve years old, trying to figure out how to masturbate to a Playboy magazine I stole from my neighbor's garage.

I was annoyed and frustrated, and the experience didn't instill a lot of self-confidence in my sexual prowess. I was glad to see my libido was still intact despite all the antidepressants and muscle relaxers the doctors had me on. It was, however, a grim reminder that sex was never going to be the same. James came back in the room about an hour later and asked me how it went. I just told him she wanted too much money.

The two of us got back on the road the next day, and James suggested we visit the Hoover Dam since we were there. Unfortunately, that turned out to be a pointless trip, at least for me it was. The wall surrounding the dam where all the visitors go was too high for me to see over. Obviously, the engineers did not consider people in wheelchairs when constructing the viewing area. James picked me up under the arms so I could catch a glimpse, but that lasted a few short seconds.

Vegas is supposed to be Sin City and a place of temptation, but for me, it was the city of exclusion. The last time I visited Vegas a few months prior to my accident I was with some co-workers from the insurance company. At that time, I exited the plane and the guys took me right to a prominent strip club at 9:00 a.m. We stayed until midnight, and I left with a gorgeous burette who took me clubbing and dancing all night. She not only payed for drinks, she insisted on coming to my hotel with no strings attached. That whole trip I partied, gambled, danced, and hooked up with a beautiful girl every night. Best vacation ever.

This time around, I was nearly thrown from an amusement ride 1200 feet in the air, paid $300 to kiss a hooker, rolled around the Vegas strip aimlessly, and saw a stupid dam. That was not the vacation I envisioned when James and I enthusiastically planned our road trip in my room a few days prior.

That Vegas experience with James was demoralizing to say the least. I felt irrelevant, unattractive, nothing but a useless invalid. Talk about a fall from grace. Escaping Minnesota and taking that trip to Vegas proved detrimental to my mental state—certainly not the escape, encouragement, and refuge I was imagining. The drive home made things even worse. Twenty-four hours to think about how bad my life actually sucked.

When we finally arrived back home, I was exhausted and dejected. I gave James the next few days off, figuring we needed a break after being cooped up in his small car together for so long. The last few hours before we entered Minnesota he wanted to pull over and sleep, and I just wanted to get the hell out of that car. We started arguing about stopping and I demanded he take me home, which made him extremely unhappy with me.

Ultimately, the trip did get me out of the house and my comfort zone, but it was another sad reminder of the life I was missing. We probably should have just stayed in Colorado or visited the Grand Canyon. Considering how I lived before paralysis, going to a party city like Las Vegas when I couldn't party completely left me on the outside looking in, and horribly rejected. It was a harsh reminder that my once perfect life was officially gone forever.

CHAPTER THIRTEEN

❖ ❖ ❖ ❖ ❖ ❖ ❖ ❖ ❖

Metamorphosis

ROUGHLY NINE MONTHS HAD PASSED since my accident and spring had finally arrived, along with warmer weather, and it was nice to finally get out onto my deck and feel the warm sun on my face. Being cooped up all day during the winter was literally driving me insane. My friends started coming over to hang out with me during the day, and we would drink beer, smoke weed, and play Battleship on my computer. It was a nice break from the monotony of boredom that filled my days during the cold season.

My PCA, James, was also getting burned out between his jobs, family, and other responsibilities, and grievously informed me he was quitting. I understood completely, but I was sad to see him go. We had formed a close friendship while he took care of me for the last six months, and I was truly grateful for his help and patience. Luckily for me, my sister took the job after James, so at least it was a rather smooth transition.

One day a few friends came by and we all went outside to chill on the deck. One of my friends was an avid hunter and outdoorsman, and whenever he came by, he would grab the BB gun in my garage and just shoot at things for fun. That day, I had gone back into my room to talk with my other friend when I heard a shot ring out and then a loud thump. I wheeled outside onto the deck and saw a dead squirrel lying on my ramp.

I just sat there in my chair, staring at the large squirrel lying in a pool of blood. I started to get a slight pain in my chest and felt sick to my stomach.

"C'mon, dude! Why the fuck did you do that?" I complained.

"Because it's fun," my friend replied, still laughing proudly at his kill. "Look at that shot. Right between the eyes."

"Clean that shit up, man. That's not cool."

My friend grabbed a piece of newspaper to pick the squirrel up by the tail and then tossed it into a small wooded area at the end of my alley. My two friends hung out for a little while longer, and I tried to act as if everything was fine, but deep down inside, all I could think about was the squirrel he had killed. Once the two of them left, I wheeled back inside and tried to just go about my day, but I couldn't get that image of the squirrel out of my head.

For nearly a month, my mind was fixated on the death of that squirrel to the point where I cried over its death and even dreamed about it at night. I was distressed over the whole event, and for a long time the feeling wouldn't go away. I kept thinking about the squirrel's life, how it just wanted to gather nuts, run around the tree branches, make baby squirrels, and live in peace.

It didn't matter that it was a squirrel—it could have been any animal for that matter. My whole issue was with the fact my friend had senselessly robbed that animal of the only life it would ever have. It seemed so unfair, and I was having difficulty with the fact that I couldn't forget about that squirrel when there were obviously more important issues to worry about in the world.

It was that single incident with the squirrel and the subsequent month of depression I had because of it that made me realize what a profound impact my accident had made on me. I had a newfound appreciation for life. That squirrel's death also made me recognize my significant love for animals and respect for all living things: insects, trees, plants, etc. I soon realized the sanctity of life had taken on a whole new meaning for me.

Before my accident, I took so many things for granted, and unfortunately, it took a traumatic, life-changing accident to make me comprehend just how special and precious life is. I started watching videos on the internet about the horrors of factory farming and even began to feel guilty about eating meat. I really became conflicted on these issues.

My preoccupation with the subject only continued as my mind was constantly consumed with thoughts of life and death and what role God played in all of this. I'd be sitting in my recliner watching the news as my mom cooked dinner, and I would start to cry over a story of a teenager being killed in a random car accident. Then there were the ads. It didn't matter if it was some feed-the-children charity or a commercial for the Humane Society; I was completely heart-broken and distraught over the suffering that animals and people endured in the world.

What kind of deity would let this happen? Why do bad things happen to good people? I wanted to believe in God and heaven, but then I would see on TV or read in the newspaper about all the terrible and unfortunate accidents that happen to innocent people every day in our society, and I just became even more confused.

I couldn't believe how much I was changing physically, mentally, emotionally, and spiritually, going through my own stages of meta-morphosis. I would like to say the experience was enlightening, but at that time, it was transforming my whole outlook on life faster than I could process it. My thoughts were literally driving me insane.

I had to talk with somebody and get some answers to these questions, or at least an explanation that made sense to me. When I went and talked with a therapist, she told me these were questions for a priest, which I thought was rather amusing. Regardless, I suppose it wasn't her area of expertise, so I called my now-retired priest from my mom's church, and he agreed to meet me for lunch one afternoon.

I told him how my mind was consumed with thoughts about death and God all the time. I asked why so many prayers go unanswered and why God allows so much suffering in the world. Father Perry was gentle, caring, and I could tell he had spent many years consoling hundreds of people asking the exact same questions just like me.

With a heavy Greek accent balanced by concise, articulate speech, Father Perry told me about the book of Job in the Bible. Job was a man bestowed with prosperity and countless blessings, but then he lost everything. He lost his wealth, family, and health, but he never cursed God. Eventually, he was rewarded for his steadfast faith, and God returned everything to him.

When I told Father Perry I didn't see the point in prayer because so many go unanswered, he told me that some prayers travel higher than others and explained why some are answered and others are not. He explained that while God may not cure my paralysis, that didn't necessarily mean He wasn't listening. The support and love from my friends and family could be a blessing, as could the return of feeling and movement below my level of injury, or the fact that I survived my ordeal at all.

I met with Father Perry multiple times. He made a lot of sense and was always insightful. I enjoyed our conversations thoroughly, and it brought me some semblance of peace. I specifically liked how he didn't tell me that my accident was God's plan or that things always happen for a reason like so many idiots would say to me out in public. I may not have been given direct answers to my questions, but I don't believe there are direct answers. Additionally, I thought he may be right in his assertion that my prayers were going unanswered because I never even acknowledged God before my accident but now was looking for Him to fix me.

I also believed that Father Perry was right in suggesting that my prayers and the prayers of others for me may be getting answered in less obvious ways. Several fundraisers were held for me by my friends, family, and even co-workers, and the love and support were overwhelming. It showed me just how much people cared for me, and how friends and family that truly care for you are the greatest blessing on earth.

I wanted more from God, though. In situations like mine, people often turn to religion or spirituality when they can't quite come to grips with a traumatic event or with the insurmountable problems in their life. That's what I was doing then. The doctors had all told me my paralysis was permanent, and since there was no medical solution, I had started to look for a miracle.

I couldn't wrap my mind around the fact that my looks, body, and athletic ability were gone forever. The amount of loss I was experiencing was akin to losing a family member or loved one. I was grieving, and this constant reflection on life, death, and religion was consuming my every thought. With nowhere else to turn, I started reading the Bible in my quest for guidance.

Unfortunately, reading the Bible didn't help much. I read a story about Jesus curing a paralyzed man and wept in my bed all night, confused yet still hopeful. All the content regarding demons and the devil only resulted in nightmares and extremely vivid dreams. I began having the same recurring nightmares as well. I kept seeing the same faceless demon consuming my body, causing me to wake in sheer terror—and the dreams got progressively worse!

One night, I suddenly awoke from a bad dream and saw a man sitting on the edge of my bed. I rubbed my eyes, trying to erase the vision, but the man remained sitting there, staring at me as I screamed like a little girl. My mom came running into my room, fumbling around for the light switch and asking me what was wrong. I told her there was a man sitting on the edge of my bed, and she thought I was nuts.

My mom calmed me down and reminded me over and over it was just a dream, but the visions continued. A few days later, I awoke from a nightmare and saw the Grim Reaper standing at the end of my bed holding his sickle. Once again, I cried out to my mother. The worst vision occurred after a similar nightmare, and when I opened my eyes, there was an image of a man floating a few feet above me, wearing a hospital mask and sharpening a butcher's knife. I was mortified!

I cried out to my mom, who came running into my room frustrated and annoyed. As I cried and described the image of the man with the knife, she told me she was going to get me a touch lamp next to my bed. I knew the visions I was having were only dreams, but they were so clear and visible in the dark. I couldn't keep going through this. I felt like the star in the A Nightmare on Elm Street movies, just waiting for Freddy fucking Krueger to murder me in my sleep.

My mother purchased a touch lamp to put next to my bed so I could turn on the lights as soon as I awoke to these visions. Thankfully, they didn't happen every night, but they occurred at least a few times a month, which was more than enough. Now, instead of waking up my mom with my screaming, I could just reach over and touch the lamp and the images would disappear instantly.

The dreams still made for a restless night, though, and they were affecting my ability to get a good night's rest. Sleep was imperative to my health at that time. My body needed it to heal, it was a reprieve from the physical pain I dealt with constantly, and it was supposed to be an escape from the mental anguish I endured all day. The nightmares and visions, however, kept turning a peaceful night's sleep into my own little horror flick.

My psychologist informed me a side effect of one of my medications was vivid dreams, but even she conceded the visions were abnormal. Because the dreams and hallucinations were religious in nature, she suggested I talk with a clergy member or somebody involved with a church. With nowhere else to turn, my aunt suggested to my mom that a priest come out and bless our house. It may sound a bit unorthodox, but at that point, I was desperate.

I called the priest from my mom's church and told him about my nightmares and visions. Priests are rather devout individuals, and after hearing about the demons haunting my dreams, he agreed a blessing was in order. It turned out these types of rituals were actually a common practice in the church and weren't much different than burning sage to cleanse a new house or place of living.

The priest came over one afternoon while my parents were at work. He sat down at our kitchen table with his briefcase and asked me to tell him more about what had been going on. I told him I was struggling with coming to terms with my disability. I was always thinking about God and religion and having recurring nightmares and hallucinations. The priest counseled me briefly and then explained exactly what he'd be doing and why a blessing of my house was in order.

He then got up from the table and opened up his briefcase, removing a large gold crucifix and several other religious accessories. He asked me for a bowl of water and said a few different prayers. After blessing the water, the priest splashed it around the house while reading from the Bible out loud and in Greek.

I didn't know what he was saying, but it reminded me a lot of the movie The Exorcist. Regardless, I didn't care how weird this all seemed. I was sick of the nightmares and would have drunk goat's blood if the priest told me it would get rid of my visions. I allowed the ritual to continue uninterrupted and didn't ask any questions.

After the priest finished the blessing of our house, I felt refreshed and had a revived spirit and belief that my sins had been expelled along with the demons that had taken up residency in my home. I was so confused since my accident when it came to religion and God, but at that moment, I was truly hopeful the blessing would work.

My mom came home from work later in the evening and asked if our priest had been by. I told her yes, the house was blessed. When I went to bed later that night, I got the best night of sleep I had had in weeks. There were no nightmares, no demons, and best yet, no visions—not that night, or the next, or that entire week, or that month. Whatever our priest did was successful—even if it was just placebo.

Summer had arrived, and it was quickly approaching the two-year anniversary of my accident. I had yet to regain any more movement despite the two-year window the doctors kept reminding me about. It didn't matter, though, because I didn't expect some miraculous recovery at that point, and I had a renewed faith in God after the blessing of my house relieved me of my nightmares and negative thoughts.

Maybe the good Lord was looking out for me in some small way, and even if He wasn't, I wasn't thinking about suicide or life and death anymore. I wasn't constantly questioning God's actions or his influence here on earth. The blessing, communion, holy water, and subsequent absence of demons in my dreams and visions in my room brought me some peace and comfort for once since my accident.

I finally concluded all my negativity and obsession with life and death were impeding my ability to move on from my accident and problems. I was fed up with how I was living and was ready for a change. I was sick of always being stuck at home, having to rely on Metro Mobility or my friends to drive me someplace. I was tired of not having money, I hated living at home with my parents, and I was done feeling depressed all the time. I knew I could do so much better with myself.

I wanted to drive on my own, I wanted to go back to work, and I wanted to move out on my own soon. I wanted the freedom and independence the rest of my friends enjoyed. I didn't like the way I looked—all pale and skinny. I yearned for whatever part of my old self I could possibly salvage.

I had a great support system around me with a very loving family and the best friends a guy could ask for. I knew they all had my back and would be more than happy and willing to help me anyway they could. Yes, my life did suck most of the time, but I wasn't going to be walking again anytime soon, so there was only one thing left to do, and that was move on from my accident.

I remembered a famous line from Andy Dufresne in one of my favorite movies, The Shawshank Redemption: "You can get busy living, or you can get busy dying!"

I certainly became more in tune spiritually and aware of the significance of theology issues I had never given a second thought to before my disability. I also knew God wasn't going to personally intervene in my life and fix my multitude of problems. If I wanted to change, it was up to me—and me only! So, I decided to get busy living.

CHAPTER FOURTEEN

◆ ◆ ◆ ◆ ◆ ◆ ◆ ◆ ◆

Brushing off the Dust

WITH SUMMER UPON US, I started lying out in the sun to get some color again. I instructed my sister to set up the fan and lounge chair on our deck for me so I could lie in the sun for a couple of hours. Because of my spinal cord injury, I could no longer sweat, so the fan was vital to keep me from overheating. The sun felt good on my joints, and the vitamin D was surprisingly effective at alleviating the seasonal depression.

One afternoon, my former hair stylist came and cut my hair since I could no longer make it to her salon. James used to take me there and carry me up the stairs leading into her workplace. Since he had quit, though, I had let my hair get out of control and a bit scraggly. Once I had a new haircut, I started shaving my body hair as well, like I did before my accident. I was taking back my manhood.

Tanning, grooming—this was all part of the big picture, the plan I had put into place to start living a happy and productive life again. It started with my appearance, trying to get back the good looks that I felt I had lost since getting released from the hospital. The next step was getting a van so I could start driving again, which would hopefully give me back some of the freedom the paralysis had robbed me of.

Once I had the van, I was going to start looking for a job and then hopefully find a gym I could use to start working out the muscles I still had use of. It may seem vain but being a quadriplegic doesn't exactly instill the greatest amount of confidence in you, and having to be in a wheelchair doesn't do wonders for your self-image either.

Society has stereotypes for people with disabilities, and I just wanted to do everything I could to break those stereotypes. The depression I was battling stole my self-worth, and I was attempting to package myself in a hip manner again to bring it back. Just because I was in a wheelchair didn't mean I couldn't be stylish and fresh. Sure, my muscles were paralyzed, but my sense of fashion remained well intact.

Therefore, I planned a shopping date to the mall with a couple of girlfriends of mine. I was going to use some of the money I had received from the fundraisers to replenish my wardrobe because my body size had drastically changed, and clothing fits differently when you're sitting in a wheelchair. I needed to get pants and jeans two inches longer like Pete had advised me, along with loose-fitted shirts that would allow me to push my wheelchair more freely.

I headed to the mall with my friends later that day. Normally I enjoyed shopping for clothes, but it didn't take long before I started to become frustrated with my disability. Whether it was trying to maneuver between the racks of clothing or not being able to try on any of the clothes because I was stuck in the wheelchair, it was becoming frustratingly clear that even something simple like shopping wouldn't come without its barriers.

I still tried to make the most of it, though. I was with good friends and had a thousand-dollar budget, so there was still a lot of fun to be had. The problem was I was picking out specific looks and styles based on my preferences before my accident and not necessarily outfits that were practical to my life with a disability.

I knew I needed to buy my pants two inches longer, but I had no idea what my waistline measured. The only thing I could do at the time was guess. Nevertheless, we visited a multitude of departments and raided endless shelves and racks until all my money was gone and we couldn't carry any more bags.

The girls and I got some food and drinks before we headed back home. When we arrived at my house, they helped me organize my new clothes and put them away in my closet and drawers. When my mom got home later that evening, she helped me try on some of the clothes I had just purchased.

It was a good thing I kept the tags on because hardly anything fit correctly. I was pissed off and started to cry out of pure frustration. My pants could be tailored, but I was going to have to return everything else and start all over. My mother, always the one to point out the positive, reminded me that on the bright side, I got to go shopping again. As usual, she was right, and a small grin appeared across my face.

The following Monday, my sister came over bright and early for my appointment with Vocational Rehabilitation Services. They would help me find a job or go back to college, and even help pay for a van if it was used to get to work or school. They provide invaluable services for people with disabilities, and I was thankful to live in a state that had such considerable resources. It was a very productive meeting, and I left there feeling extremely encouraged about my future.

Now that I knew Vocational Rehab would help pay for a handi-cap conversion for an accessible vehicle, I decided to start the process of looking for a van. After doing some research, I found a place in Savage, Minnesota, that did the van conversions in my state. I made an appointment for later in the week, and my father and I went and visited the facility.

I wasn't too thrilled with having to drive a van. I typically associated them with soccer moms and kidnappers. However, after looking at some of the models, I was surprised by how cool they appeared. I was also shocked by the price tag—nearly $40,000 for some of them—and was even more thankful that the state was going to help cover some of the cost.

With my new van ordered, the day had arrived for my driving lesson at the local rehab center. I showed up for my appointment, and a little old guy came and got me from the waiting area and escorted me to the garage where the test vehicle sat. The instructor pushed a button, and the door opened automatically while the ramp unfolded.

I wheeled up to the minivan, which was similar to the one I'd be getting, and he pushed me up the ramp and into the driver's seat.

The instructor strapped my wheelchair down and then gave me some brief instructions. He told me to pull back on the hand controls to accelerate and push forward to brake. He then opened the garage door and pointed to the road.

"Just like that?" I asked. "No flight simulators, testing, classwork, etc.?"

"No, sir," the instructor answered nonchalantly. "Just pull back on that to go."

I was a little taken aback at first. I had figured there were going to be intense classroom tutorials before ever getting behind the wheel. The instructor told me, though, that driving was simple, and I wouldn't require all that classroom instruction. He could tell by my physicality that I could handle the vehicle just fine.

Trusting his expertise, I hit the gas and went soaring out of the garage and into the street like a NASCAR driver. The hand controls and power steering were very sensitive, and I hadn't anticipated how fast the van would accelerate. I slammed on the brakes, and the two of us lurched forward violently.

"Holy shit! These controls are sensitive," I said in shock.

"Yeah, or you're too strong," he joked back.

This time, I pulled back on the gas gently, and off we went. It felt great to be behind the wheel again. For the first time in a while, I felt like a normal human being, driving down the road with the window down and the breeze in my face.

I asked the instructor if I could turn on the radio, and he agreed. The sun was shining through the window while the music played, and for a short moment, I forgot I was even sitting in a wheelchair. I got lost in the newfound freedom I was experiencing. I no longer felt trapped. In fact, I briefly felt like I was cruising in my CRX on the way to the gym or work, just like before my accident, but that feeling was short-lived as I had to carefully navigate the hand controls on the van.

Soon after my driving course, I got a call from the sales rep at the conversion center telling me the handicap conversion on my van was complete. My dad and I drove up there the following day. When I wheeled into the garage and saw the van for the first time, I was ecstatic.

There she was—a little red sport minivan with ground effects and a lowered suspension. It looked surprisingly cool. People probably wouldn't think I was a creepy pervert in that thing, and I might even pick up some chicks.

When I was discharged from the hospital, I had felt extremely anxious and worried, comparing my situation to a baby bird leaving its nest too soon without the ability to fly. With my new van, I again felt like a bird leaving its nest—but now, I had a fresh pair of wings allowing me to soar around society independently.

It was empowering, and I felt like a normal kid again, able to go run a quick errand or meet up with my friends on a moment's notice. The only remaining impediment was my inability to get back into my house on my own once I left. I could go down the ramp that we built in the backyard by myself, but it was far too steep for me to wheel up without somebody pushing from behind.

My case worker recommended a few different organizations that could possibly help, and I made some calls. We found one group that offered to donate a stair climber, the kind that is generally used by elderly people to get up and down stairs. My parents and I weren't sure how it was going to solve my problem, but we weren't going to pass up such a valuable resource.

Fortunately, my parents worked with a lady whose husband was an engineer. He came over to the house one day and examined the chair lift, and then devised a plan to attach it to the stairs of our outside deck. He also welded a platform to it so I could just wheel my chair right onto the thing. He was an intelligent guy, and when he completed the assembly, the lift worked perfectly. Now I was truly free.

Freedom and independence—I use those two words quite often when discussing my life. That's because your freedom and independence are the first things to go after a paralyzing accident, and those are the two biggest things you desperately look to regain as you try to pick up the pieces of a shattered life. I got a van allowing me the freedom to travel most anywhere I wanted to at any time, and now with the lift installed on my house I could finally come and go independently as well.

I put a stereo system and subwoofer in my van a few weeks after taking ownership of it, and that was the icing on the cake. I felt revived and energetic, and to say my emotional well-being had improved leaps and bounds would be an understatement. I felt like Humpty Dumpty—gradually getting put back together again with every productive step I took forward.

My doctor noticed a significant change in my mood as well, and that's when I told her I wanted to stop taking my antidepressant because I didn't feel like I needed it anymore. I still had thoughts about the loss of my legs and body, and all the sports and activities I could no longer participate in, but I didn't dwell on it like I use to. I would think about it, grieve for a bit, and then move on.

Now I concentrated more on the positives, and that was the key. When things got bad, I would concentrate on the good, like how much function I had, how lucky I was to have a nice vehicle, and all my good friends and family. Thinking about what I had and not what I lost made a big difference. If I was feeling down, I would go for a drive and listen to music. Positive thinking and being productive— these were essential to my recovery.

CHAPTER FIFTEEN

◆ ◆ ◆ ◆ ◆ ◆ ◆ ◆ ◆

A Return to Normalcy

THREE YEARS AFTER MY ACCIDENT, my attitude had improved so much that my doctor asked if I'd like to participate in the Think First Program, speaking at schools about my accident. The program was apparently started by a group of neurosurgeons and doctors who were becoming alarmed over the number of young people sustaining brain and spinal cord injuries. Many of these incidents are preventable and alcohol-related, so the program's main objective was injury prevention through education.

I would be working with a paramedic that discussed first response, a nurse that explained the medical and rehabilitation side of sustaining a traumatic injury, and then somebody who had actually been injured, such as myself. Immediately I agreed, feeling that maybe this was my calling. Even if it wasn't, it would allow me the opportunity to turn my accident into a positive thing and perhaps make a difference in young people's lives.

With a new school year underway, my first speaking engagement came up quickly. I had been practicing what I was going to say, but I hadn't prepared any written notecards. I wanted to speak from the heart for the most part. I was scheduled to speak all day to several different health classes, and as my mom helped me get ready early that morning, I was growing increasingly anxious and scared.

I had never done public speaking before, and the thought of being up in front of a lot of students in my wheelchair was a bit nerve-wrecking. I started to cry and told my mom I didn't want to go, but she calmed me down and kept reminding me of the importance of the program and what we were doing. The nurse and the paramedic I was meeting there were counting on me showing up, so I couldn't just ditch them. I collected my composure and tried to concentrate on the bigger picture, and then I got in my van and drove to the high school.

I arrived at the school just in time for the start of the class and introduced myself to the nurse and paramedic I'd be working with. When the program started, the paramedic went up first and gave his presentation, incorporating a neck brace and even strapping a student to a trauma board to demonstrate what first responders do. The nurse went up next and talked about all the messed-up kids she's had to care for over the course of her career as a registered nurse. Then it was my turn.

I wheeled up to the front of the large class—about fifty students—and all eyes were on me. Everything I had rehearsed at home was out the door—I'd forgotten everything I had prepared to say. I was extremely nervous and just kind of sat there like a deer in the headlights trying to figure out where to start. Finally, I decided to tell my story just like it happened.

"It wasn't that long ago I sat in the same chairs you guys are sitting in now, listening to some guy in a wheelchair lecture me about the dangers of drugs and alcohol," I began. "I was young, popular, athletic, good-looking, and had a great life, just like all of you."

I could tell by the looks on the students' faces that I had their attention, so I decided to keep on going, just speaking from the heart. I spoke to them about my perfect life and how it all had been taken away from me forever because I didn't think about the depth of the water before I dove into it.

"I was drunk, having fun, and being irresponsible, and my poor decision cost me the use of most of my body," I somberly informed the kids. "Now I'm paralyzed forever."

I told the kids to imagine themselves sitting in their desks for the rest of their lives. That was what my life had become.

"My wheelchair is my prison, and I'd been given a life sentence!" I exclaimed. "We only get one shot at life, one chance to live on earth and enjoy all its beauty, our family, friends, favorite activities. Imagine it all ripped from you in a split second—gone forever—then spending the rest of your life on earth paralyzed, a vegetable, or even dead under the ground." I reminded the students, "It can happen to you as easily as it did me."

I wasn't very articulate, and I may have been a little redundant, but I was sincere and impassioned. As I kept talking, I could feel the tears running down my face, but I didn't wipe them away. I continued to explain how difficult it was to deal with a spinal cord injury and paralysis. I wanted them all to feel my pain, and more importantly, to recognize that what happened to me could happen to them.

From the look on most people's faces, I don't believe anyone expected such a heartfelt speech about our choices in life and the potential ramifications. I wiped the tears from my face and apologized for getting upset, but I also reminded them not to take life for granted. As I looked around the room, there wasn't a dry eye in the class.

"I thought I was invincible," I told the students. "I never imagined my life like this when I was you."

As the day progressed, the more I spoke, the more I improved. I added some jokes and humor to lighten the mood but kept the passion and emotion to really get across my point. I cried a few more times in some of the other classes, but it only helped further drive home the message I attempted to convey.

The detailed description of the night of my accident was physically bothering some of the students, even the teacher's aide. One student vomited at his desk and another had to leave the class, but the teacher's assistant took it the worst. As I was giving my speech, I noticed he was having trouble standing. I asked if he was OK, but he assured me he was fine even though his face was white as a ghost, so I proceeded along. Suddenly, he stumbled towards the exit and passed out, falling and cracking his head open on the ground.

There was a lot of blood, but after he regained consciousness, I couldn't help but giggle. Thankfully, there were a nurse and a paramedic in the classroom, but I couldn't believe my story was so upsetting—either that or he was in the wrong field of study. How ironic that during a speech about injury prevention, I caused a major injury. Regardless, I wasn't going to tone my message down.

My intensity energized the nurse and paramedic I spoke with, and together, we made a formidable team. We took pride in what we were doing, and it honestly felt like we were making a difference. At the end of the day, the teacher was very appreciative that we had come out and said she was going to ask us back once the new semester started. As the three of us were leaving, various students came up to us and expressed their gratitude as well.

I booked speaking engagements on a regular basis after that, which was nice because it provided me with some extra money. The speaking engagements didn't pay a lot, but when I combined that with living at home rent-free, I finally had some money to go along with my van and my newfound freedom, and I started getting out with my friends on a regular basis.

I was much more confident in public more than I had been right after my accident. I was tan, had new clothes and a nice vehicle, and wasn't nearly as depressed as before. I was acting like the pre-injury Eric: outgoing and extroverted. At the bars and clubs, I started getting on the dance floor again. I didn't really give a shit what I looked like, waving my arms around and trying to dance.

I was personable, carefree, and appreciative of the fact that I could go out in such a capacity. I was even getting approached by girls who appreciated I was still living my life to the fullest, a much-welcomed and dearly-missed aspect of my previous life before my accident.

The more pieces of a productive life that fell into place for me, the more I felt I was becoming a normal member of society again. I was going everywhere I could go in my van, and people's perception of me was no longer a concern. I was really learning to shrug things off, and to be quite honest, I was having very positive experiences with strangers and people I didn't know when out in public.

I believe a lot of this had to do with my attitude and appearance. I was trying to follow the advice Pete gave me in the hospital about breaking stereotypes, and it was really paying dividends. Sometimes people would pay for my food or drinks, and elderly ladies would even give me money, which I didn't need but never said no to. I was always extremely courteous and grateful, saying thank you and acknowledging the kind gestures with a big smile.

People were even more kind and giving in the clubs and bars. That's a big reason the bars became my oasis—my escape, you could argue. They were a place where I forgot about my problems and focused my energy on having a good time with my friends. Yes, there was binge drinking involved, but I liked how alcohol made me feel. It gave me courage to go back out on the dance floor with everybody else and not care what they thought. It made conversations more amusing, increased my patience, and even got rid of the burning pain that I was always experiencing in my back. The whole environment and atmosphere could numb all my pain, both physical and emotional. I just didn't think about my paralysis when I was busy laughing and partying with my friends, and that's why I started going out a lot more.

Nightclubs and bars were also where the girls hung out, and my newly discovered confidence and zeal for life were garnering attention from the ladies. Girls started approaching me frequently and would straddle my lap on the dance floor or just ask questions about my accident. Even when they were being overly flirtatious, though, I still wasn't quite comfortable asking any of them out.

That all changed one night when some friends and I were drinking at one of our local hangouts. I noticed a cute girl staring at me all night from across the bar. We made eye contact throughout the evening, and then, toward the end of the night, she came over and started hanging all over me. She sat on my lap, pretty much throwing herself at me, and before long, the two of us were making out.

I introduced myself, and she told me her name was Amy. We flirted, kissed, and joked around for the rest of the night. This girl obviously didn't have a problem with my disability, and I was perfectly content with that. Even though I was hesitant at first, I built up the courage to ask her out, and she gave me her phone number with an emphatic yes.

Amy and I met up later that week and started to hang out a lot thereafter. It turned out we had mutual friends, and soon after, our groups were going to the same bars and house parties, which made dating her that much more enjoyable. We always had a great time together. I did my best to stay positive at all times and tried to make her feel as comfortable as possible with my disability.

Amy was home from college for the summer, and I wasn't working other than speaking engagements once or twice a week, so we spent a lot of time together during the day. Both of our parents were gone during the day, so that's when we had either house all to ourselves. One day, Amy and I were making out in her bed, and I figured it was time to take our brief relationship to the next level.

We'd been dating a few weeks now, and I could tell she wanted to have sex, but I was still apprehensive. It was like being a virgin again but much worse, because when you're a guy, you want to lose your virginity. This time around, though, I was terrified about not being able to perform or satisfy Amy sexually. I figured it was time to get it over with, though, and kept concentrating on what I had learned from the prostitute in Vegas.

As Amy sat on top of me grinding up and down, I could feel I was erect and blurted out, "Do you want to have sex?" I wanted to seize the moment before it was gone.

I could tell by the look on Amy's face the answer was yes. She took off her shorts and then helped me pull mine down before getting on top of me, and just like that, I was having sex. It felt great, and I was really attracted to Amy, so now I was just praying I'd maintain an erection long enough for her liking. I couldn't ejaculate, and my sexual function was impaired just like my bladder and bowel function, so I had no idea how long I could keep going.

My psychologist was right about the emotional connection that I would experience. After going at it for several minutes, I started to feel a sense of relief. I had just gotten over another one of my hurdles and conquered another fear—one of my greatest fears since my accident. The sex was surprisingly good for me, and Amy appeared to enjoy herself, too.

After we were done, we lay together for a while, and that's when she started to ask me several questions about my physical capabilities. We had a long conversation, and I just put all my cards on the table and was honest about everything. Amy was very nonchalant about my situation, and my disability didn't seem to bother her at all.

Amy was a smart girl and very open-minded. Out of anybody I could have had sex with for the first time after my accident, I'm glad it was her. Now that we had broken the ice, we started having sex more frequently, and one time, I could tell I gave her an orgasm, something she told me had never happened to her before. Knowing that I could still sexually gratify women provided me with the final key to that feeling of normalcy that I had assumed was lost forever.

IV

◆ ◆ ◆ ◆ ◆ ◆ ◆ ◆ ◆

DOWNWARD SPIRAL

CHAPTER SIXTEEN

◆ ◆ ◆ ◆ ◆ ◆ ◆ ◆ ◆

Collision Course

I FELT MY LIFE WAS improving, and I was making positive strides, but oh, how quickly things changed. A friend of the family came over one day with a VHS tape she had from a barbeque shortly before my accident. She thought I'd like to have the video because it showed me before my time as a quadriplegic. I don't know why she thought I'd like to see that, but her intentions were in the right place, so I just put the video on my desk in my room and thanked her for bringing it over.

Later that evening, Amy came to my house to watch a movie and hang out, and she asked me what was on the tape. After I told her it was me before my paralysis, she begged to watch it. I was very hesitant, worried about the emotions it could trigger, but Amy wanted to see me before my days in a wheelchair. I begrudgingly agreed.

As soon as we put the tape in and pressed play, the video showed me getting out of my beloved car with a hot girl. My shirt was off and my muscles were bulging. My little nieces and nephews ran into my arms as I tossed them in the air, catching them on their way down like I did when I lived with them all.

"Uncle, uncle, uncle, do me next!"

"No, me first!" they demanded innocently.

I tossed my nephew in the air as the girl I was with introduced herself to my family. My mom gave me a big hug, and my dad looked on with pride. The video was a little grainy, but you could still see my face brimming with joy, happiness, and complete contentment.

I could barely watch the video, and when I looked over at Amy, I could see a look on her face like she was missing out.

"You would have never dated me before your accident, would you?" she asked, upset.

"I don't know—I was very superficial, I'm not going to lie," I admitted honestly. "I definitely would have banged you, if that's any consolation."

I tried to play it cool during the video, but after a couple of minutes, the tears started flowing, and I was overcome with grief. Distraught, I demanded the video be turned off immediately. I knew that would happen, and despite Amy's best efforts to console me, I politely asked her to leave. I wanted to be left alone.

What I saw in that video became etched in my memory, and I noticed I was dwelling on it obsessively over the next week or so. I tried to suppress those thoughts, acting as if everything was fine, but slowly, those memories just turned into a bundle of dry tinder inside my soul. The more I repressed the memories and feelings, the dryer the tinder became.

I started to go out even more than I did before I saw the video, trying to keep my mind occupied with happy thoughts as I drank and partied with my friends. Around that same time, I started to notice how much more prevalent cocaine was becoming with a certain group of friends I was hanging with quite often. Gradually, I began to increase my own use of the drug. I kept telling myself it was all in good fun, but deep down, I had feelings and issues that were fueling my desire to numb my senses. I kept trying to focus on the positives, like Amy and my van, but even all of that was about to change.

One night, I was at the bar drinking with some friends when Amy called me up and invited me over. She had a cousin in town, and they were all hanging out with her parents. I loved Amy's family— they were kind, caring, and a lot of fun to be around—so I told my friends I'd catch them later and drove to Amy's parents' house. When I arrived, Amy introduced me to her cousin and cousin's fiancé, and we all chilled on their deck drinking wine.

It started to get late, but instead of ending the festivities, we decided to make our way to a nearby bar for a nightcap. The four of us jumped into my van and made our way to the dive bar, which was no more than a half mile from Amy's parents' place. At the bar, we had a couple more drinks and did shots until it was closing time.

As we got ready to leave, it started to rain heavily, and I noticed Amy's cousin was a little apprehensive about getting in my van. I assured them all I was completely fine to drive, though, and reminded them that Amy's house was only two minutes away.

We all got into my van, but as we drove down the road, I could barely see a few feet in front of me. My windshield wipers were on full speed as the wind and rain pounded against my van like a hurricane in full force. I tried my absolute best to concentrate on what was directly in front of me, but as we approached a bend in the road, my van started to fishtail. I turned my steering wheel to compensate, but it was too late—I lost control. The last thing I heard was Amy saying, "Oh, no," and then a very loud crash.

When the dust from the airbags began to settle—literally—I could see I was in a ditch. We had plowed straight into a large tree. All the neighborhood dogs started barking as numerous porch lights started to come on. I made sure everybody in the van was OK, which they were, thankfully, so now it was just a matter of time before the police showed. I tried to compose myself and come up with a story, but even a convincing story wasn't going to get me past a breathalyzer.

When the police officer approached my window, I tried telling him I hadn't been driving that long from a wheelchair and just lost control of my van in the rain. I did admit to having some drinks, though, and I immediately failed the breathalyzer test. I was crying and very upset. I could tell my van was destroyed, and I believe the officer took pity on me. He gave me a ticket for careless driving and released me into the care of Amy's parents, who pushed my wheelchair back to their house a couple of blocks away.

In the morning, I had to call my parents to come pick me up from Amy's house and I broke the unfortunate news to them about my van. When my dad asked me if I had been drinking, I emphatically said no, blaming the accident on the rain and road conditions. Fortunately, my van was fully insured through my parent's insurance agency, and they covered all the costs for another handicap accessible van. Still, I didn't have a vehicle for about six weeks and was still pretty upset about the whole situation.

I felt bad for Amy and was a little embarrassed that I had just met and nearly killed her cousin and cousin's fiancé that night. Overall, though, I was very lucky nobody was hurt and extremely grateful that insurance was replacing my vehicle with a newer vehicle. I ended up with a far cooler and nicer van than my previous one. Insurance even covered the cost of the handicap conversion, which nobody thought they'd do.

With a new van and my freedom restored, I felt rejuvenated, and the sorrow from watching myself on the video recording had dissipated. Things were going great, and everything seemed right in the world. As summer was ending, though, Amy dropped a bombshell on me and told me she was returning to college in a few weeks.

I knew this day was coming, but I had pretty much ignored it the entire summer while Amy and I were dating. We had never even talked about what would happen after she left. I had just assumed we'd try and do the long-distance thing, but I could tell by Amy's demeanor that she wasn't all that interested in doing that. She liked me, and we no doubt had a lot of fun together, but I think I was more of a summer fling than anything for her.

I felt sad—worse, I felt used. I was usually on the opposite end of that game, so this was a feeling I certainly wasn't accustomed to. I really liked Amy, and her family was so thoughtful and generous, I knew I was going to miss them just as much. She attended college in Wisconsin, and I volunteered to drive her and her things up there when she needed to leave. For the remaining two weeks, I tried to act as if everything was fine.

Things were far from good, though. I was getting depressed over the thought of losing her, and I didn't like the complete lack of control. Before my accident, I was the one who broke things off with girls, and they were the ones left crying. Now the tables had turned, and it was a bitter pill to swallow.

All the repressed feelings I had deep down inside me—the ones that had turned into a dry bundle of tinder—kept growing and growing, but I continued to bottle them up. I really was trying to stay positive, but it was an exercise in futility. Paralysis and depression were partners in crime. If I was dealing with one, it felt like there was no escaping the other.

I drove Amy to her college in Wisconsin, where we dropped off all her things at her apartment. I left early the next morning because I wanted to get back in time for the first Vikings game of the NFL season, but the whole way back to Minnesota, I just became more despondent. Every song that came on the radio reminded me of Amy, and I just couldn't stop thinking about my life with girls before my accident. Back then, I could have any girl I wanted, and now I didn't know if I'd ever date again. Even if I did, I still had to go through all the bullshit and paranoia about how I go to the bathroom, how I have sex, etc.

All the memories and feelings I thought I had finally gotten past were resurfacing, and it seemed like I was taking a major step backwards. Amy leaving was just the spark needed to ignite the dry tinder ball of feelings I was suppressing, and the ensuing fire would be relentless. Despite all the advances I had made, the feelings of loss and resentment were too overwhelming. My mind, heart, and soul were helpless.

I made it back to Minnesota in time for the Vikings game and met a bunch of my friends at one of our favorite local bars. I started to pound the drinks one after another, doing whatever I could to drown my sorrows in copious amounts of liquor. It wasn't long before everybody was drunk, and then we turned to cocaine to continue the fun. After the game was over, we headed back to a party house where we frequently went after bar close to carry on the festivities.

Once we were there, we got the music playing and everybody jacked up on alcohol and drugs. Everyone was having fun as we partied, laughed, and told old stories. I know it may seem sad and unfortunate, but I wasn't thinking about Amy or my past life anymore, and I wasn't depressed. I was having a great time and felt energized as I danced and conversed with my friends late into the night.

This was my escape, the way I forgot about my disability and subsequent problems, and I didn't see anything wrong with it at that time. I continued in the same manner over the next few weeks, and even though I vowed to keep my drinking to a minimum while I was driving, I broke that vow almost immediately upon my return from dropping off Amy.

I was going out a lot, trying to keep my mind preoccupied with fun, so I didn't have to deal with the grief and sadness. The fire that burned inside me raged on as I tried to pour alcohol over it to stifle the flames. I'd meet my friends at a bar and then drive everybody to some after party to do drugs. I was coming home later and later at night, and eventually earlier and earlier in the morning.

The accident with my van had set me back financially, and now I was burning through what little money I had like it was toilet paper. I started looking for a job and found part-time work with a wireless phone company doing customer service. I wasn't physically able to work full time because of various health factors, and because of the medical benefits I was receiving, I was very limited as to how much money I could make.

One morning, I read a story about a lady who won nine million dollars from McDonald's because she spilled hot coffee on herself. Why couldn't I get money from my accident? This was America—a very litigious society. We're genetically disposed to sue somebody for something eventually. Surely complete paralysis had to be worth something. There were certainly no guarantees, but I was desperate. It wouldn't hurt to look into it.

It was a decision I wasn't taking lightly. My friendship with Andy and his parents was very important to me, and the last thing I wanted was to ruin that. I conferred with a couple other good friends of mine about what I was contemplating, and they agreed it was something I should at least find out more about. My medical expenses were going to be extensive and ongoing, so whatever extra money I could get would be much needed. Furthermore, they all agreed Andy and his parents would most likely support me.

One of my good friends referred me to an attorney who was a family friend and specialized in personal injury. I made an appointment with this attorney and drove to his office a week later to discuss my situation. His name was John, and he was a great guy. He explained to me those types of cases came down to two main criteria: the severity of the injury and liability.

Obviously, my injuries were extreme, but there wasn't much liability because I was twenty-one years old at the time of my accident. If Andy's parents were letting minors drink and party at their house, then it would be a different story. We were all legal drinking age, however, so that complicated things. Regardless, John decided to take my case because he sympathized with my situation.

From there, my emotional rollercoaster ride continued despite my new job and cool van. I was slowly forgetting about Amy and working steadily at my new job, and now that school was starting again, my speaking engagements were about to pick up as well. My mind was occupied most of the time, and I didn't have too much time to dwell on the past.

One morning, as I got ready for work, I turned on the TV as I normally would and saw on the news that the World Trade Center was on fire. I called my sister into my room to show her, but nobody at that point had any concrete information as to what exactly had happened. They reported a plane had hit the building but didn't say how or what kind of plane. As I continued to watch while eating my breakfast, another plane flew into the second tower live on TV and burst into flames. My sister and I just sat there with our mouths agape in a state of shock and disbelief.

"This is a terrorist attack," I yelled angrily.

My sister and I were fixated on the coverage as we watched the buildings burning and desperate people hanging out the windows or jumping to their deaths. It was heartbreaking to witness all that death and carnage in real time. I called my job and told them I wasn't coming in that day, and they understood completely. I watched the news as the Pentagon was hit next, followed by another plane that was brought down in a field by the desperate passengers on board trying to save themselves.

I called my mom at work, crying and asking if she was watching what was happening, and she told me she was. A few minutes later, the first World Trade Center crumbled, and a few minutes later, the second followed it. I sat in my chair in shock. It was so surreal, like watching a movie.

I was devastated. I just couldn't stop thinking about the poor people on those planes and in those buildings, and what a horrible death they had all just endured. Empathy was clearly becoming my strongest attribute. The part of me that changed after my accident, the part that was so much more aware and conscious of the sanctity of life, had taken over my body as a deep state of despair and depression engulfed my mind and spirit.

I became very disheartened with the world after 9/11. The randomness of life—how we never even really know when our time is up, and how things can change in an instant—weighed on my mind every day and night. That people could wake up in the morning, kiss their children goodbye, go to their job like usual, and then have a fucking plane fly into their office and kill everybody was simply beyond my mental grasp.

For every action, there is a reaction. The more disheartened I became, the more I turned to drugs and partying to counter the darkness. I started to notice a change related to my drug use—it was taking greater amounts of cocaine to get me high. I also noticed how much more dejected I would become once I started to come down from the drug. Still, I felt it was my only escape, and I was having a great time with my friends when we partied.

Moderation was slowly turning to abuse, but I didn't recognize it. From my perspective, partying with my friends was the only thing left I could partake in because of my disability, so I was going to party to the full extent of my capabilities. I couldn't go golfing with my friends, so I'd go to the bar. If I couldn't dance with a hot girl on the dance floor, I'd do a shot of tequila. If I started to get too down on myself for whatever reason, I'd get an eight-ball of cocaine for energy and resurgence. That was how I rationalized my drug and alcohol use.

At that point, my overindulgence began to seep into my responsibilities. I started to call into work sick more frequently after pulling all-nighters, but I would always use my disability as an excuse so my employer couldn't hold it against me. I still managed to make my speaking engagements, though, refusing to let my partying interfere with my message to the students.

I started to show up to the schools hungover, sometimes even high on coke after staying up all night without sleep. I still managed to give a speech on the dangers of drugs and alcohol with a straight face. Sadly, I didn't even care I was being hypocritical. I was actually proud of myself for fulfilling my speaking obligations. Nobody could tell anyway—I was getting proficient at disguising my reality.

Questionable ethics were certainly the story of my life during that time as I cloaked myself under the veil of drinking and partying and attempted to forget about the memories of my past life, which still consumed my thoughts and feelings. I may have felt a little guilty at times for my behavior, especially when I lied to my mother, but for the most part, I didn't even think about it.

When I did think about it, I still didn't believe I was doing anything wrong, not even when I drank and drove. Because of my accident and disability, I felt entitled to self-destruct and even to break the law. This was my reasoning, the justification that I constantly used to suppress thoughts of potential consequences and remorse for my actions. I was a quadriplegic who had lost every-thing, so I could do whatever the fuck I wanted!

CHAPTER SEVENTEEN

◆ ◆ ◆ ◆ ◆ ◆ ◆ ◆ ◆

Catching Cases

I CONTINUED DOWN THE ROAD of self-medicating and self-destruction for several months. Finally, one early Sunday morning, I wheeled into the house after a two-day drug bender, feeling lower than pond scum, and told my mom everything. I'm not even sure why I decided to tell her. Part of me felt guilty because of everything she did for me, or maybe it was a cry for help. It simply felt the time to come clean about my issues was upon me.

Regardless, I was sobbing uncontrollably as I admitted all these late nights and early mornings were related to my heavy cocaine use. My mother looked disappointed but certainly not surprised—she had known something was up all along, but probably didn't know how to handle the situation given my disability and limitations.

After my admission of guilt, the typical promises were made. I promised to clean up my act, and my parents promised to take away privileges if I didn't. I even managed to stay true to my promises, at least for a while. Denial, however, is not a river in Egypt, and at that time, my family and I were drowning in it.

Whenever I went out, too much temptation surrounded me, and I gradually began to fall into the same ferocious cycle. I had an entire playbook of excuses and lies to explain why I was coming home so late, most of them rather believable.

However, things changed one morning after I had partied all night. After getting home early in the morning, I swiftly glided by my parents in the kitchen and went straight to my room, where I transferred into bed. I just laid there awake, eyes wide open because I was crashing and couldn't sleep worth shit. Suddenly, my nose started gushing blood. It was like Mike Tyson had punched me square in the nose—it wouldn't stop.

The only thing I could do was grab my pillowcase, but the blood was getting all over my sheets and bedspread, and I didn't want to call for my mom. Ultimately, I had no choice. My room was starting to look like a crime scene, and I needed help to stop the bleeding.

"Mom, I need your help, please," I yelled. "Quick!"

Annoyed, my mom made her way into my bedroom, knowing I was fucked up in some form or another. Sure enough, she took one look and knew.

"For crying out loud, Eric!" she screamed. "You're done doing this! You're getting help!"

Normally, I'd attempt to lie my way out of that scenario, but there was no explaining away a bloody nose of that nature. I kept my mouth shut except when I said sorry and thank you.

I really didn't think I was partying that hard. Yeah, we'd stay up late, but we didn't even leave the bars till two or three in the morning, so that's why I got home so late. At that moment, though, with wads of tissue packed up my nose to keep me from bleeding to death, I knew I needed to dial it back some.

"I'll go to treatment if you guys want," I told my parents.

"You're damn right you will!" My mom declared as she stuffed garbage bags full of bloodied tissues.

Later that week, I checked myself into treatment after research-ing a couple of places. I didn't believe I needed help, but I needed to appease my parents. At the very least, I figured treatment wouldn't hurt, and maybe it could help get me headed in a more positive direction. It wasn't like I was really enjoying life at the moment.

After about a week in treatment, I became completely bored and disinterested. The constant meetings and homework assignments were becoming annoying and redundant. Furthermore, most of the people in there had serious problems, worse than me, and I was the only one physically disabled. After seeing all these chronic addicts and alcoholics and hearing the stories about their messed-up lives, I truly believed I didn't belong in there. My alcohol and drug use paled in comparison to the abuse these individuals subjected themselves to.

Most of the patients in treatment were poor minorities, addicted to hardcore drugs like heroin and crack, or chronic alcoholics, like the one guy with sclerosis. I had never seen anything like that before. His skin was yellow like a banana, his stomach was swollen, and his lips were always chapped and bloody. The doctors said if he had one more sip of alcohol, it would kill him—and it did. One day he was just gone.

My problem wasn't with an addiction to drugs, I decided. I could turn it on and off whenever I wanted. I only drank at the bar and did coke at the after parties. My issues were strictly related to the loss I had endured after my accident and my inability to come to terms with my disability. Partying was my escape—drugs were simply the hors d'oeuvre. I told myself I didn't need treatment.

Furthermore, I had a real problem with the twelve-step program. I was supposed to admit that I was powerless over drugs and alcohol, which I completely disagreed with. It was my decision to drive to the bars and drink, and it was my decision to go to the after parties and do cocaine. I was in control, and only I could decide not to partake in these activities. My biggest issue, though, was with this whole notion of surrendering myself to God and having complete faith that God, and only God, could cure my addiction and restore my sanity.

I told the counselors they clearly didn't understand my contentious relationship with the almighty. I had been praying to God until I was blue in the face since my accident, asking for help. Not a single prayer had ever been answered, and now I was supposed to surrender to Him and expect Him to help me get sober? What if people didn't believe in God? Clearly there had to be addicts in society who were either atheists or agnostic. What were they supposed to do in treatment, I asked?

"Anything can represent your higher power, Eric," the counselor answered.

"Oh, really? Can I surrender all my will over to that plant?" I pointed to the plant in the corner.

She was not amused, as their strategy for sobriety was for me to trust that some invisible being or inanimate object was going to help me kick my drug and alcohol use, even though it had been completely nonexistent in every other aspect of my life. I started challenging my counselors in our meetings over these steps involving my higher power, and some of the sessions turned rather hostile.

To be honest, the counselors couldn't answer my questions other than to say these steps were part of a tried and tested process for alcohol and drug treatment. It was hard to convince me of that when I read the recidivism rate is around eighty percent. I respect the fact that the twelve steps work for some addicts, but the process wasn't something I could trust in at the time. My mind had become impervious to their form of psycho-babble.

After two weeks, I had had enough. I told my counselors that I was checking out of inpatient treatment but would continue as an outpatient. I used my disability as the primary excuse, and it definitely played a role in me wanting to leave. For the most part, though, I just didn't believe I belonged in there with those other patients. I had convinced myself I could control my drug and alcohol use, unlike those crackheads and junkies.

I actually had a great deal of respect for a lot of people in there. I made some friends I cared about and wanted to keep in contact with. Many of us shared a unique bond because of the hardships we faced in life, self-inflicted or not. They might have completely ruined their lives and done a lot of messed-up shit, but ultimately, they were good people with big hearts who just succumbed to their addiction.

It was a weekday when I left, and I got home before my parents got back from work. I decided to call my mom and tell her I checked myself out instead of surprising her when she got home. I was honest with her and told her I didn't think I belonged there, explaining how it was becoming very difficult for me to sleep and deal with my disability in that place. I assured her, though, that I had learned a lot over the last two weeks, and it had been a very enlightening experience. I also promised her I would continue to go as an outpatient.

My mom trusted me, and even though she was slightly disappointed, she really wasn't too upset I had left. She almost seemed kind of proud that I had given it a try for as long as I did. For the next two weeks, I did attend the outpatient meetings—I even gave rides to a couple of the patients I met in there who were now transitioning to outpatient care. I might have given up on treatment, but they hadn't, and it felt good to help them out as much as I could.

Eventually, I grew tired of the whole twelve-step program and the bullshit homework they gave us. One day, I just stopped going all together. I had dedicated a month of my time to the program, and it was enough time for me to reflect on the choices I continued to make and realize I needed to take my life in a different direction.

Yearning to stay out of debt and save money with my job, I behaved myself for a while. I didn't stop drinking completely, but to be honest, I didn't want to stop drinking. I still had fun at the bars and clubs with my friends, and unfortunately, that was still my escape. In the beginning, I was convinced I could keep my drinking to moderate levels, and I did for a while. Ironically, though, that's when I got arrested for my first DUI.

I went to a party early on a Saturday evening, and everybody there was shit-faced. I had only had a couple of drinks when I overheard my friends discussing another friend who was trying to get a ride over to our party. Because I was sober, I volunteered to go pick him up since nobody else there was in any shape to drive. As soon as I pulled out of the driveway, the police pulled me over. They were literally staking out the house.

I ended up blowing a point-one-zero, which was exactly the legal limit, so I thought I was in the clear. Apparently, though, you can still be charged with a DUI if you're at the legal limit, which seemed like a bit of contradiction to me. I was at the legal limit, not the illegal limit. Regardless, I was booked and processed.

Luckily, the police showed mercy on me. They were surprisingly cool and told me they wouldn't impound my van or take me to jail. The officer asked if somebody could come pick me up from the White Bear police station instead. I wasn't going to call my parents, so I called my friends at the party. It was too late.

I hung up the phone and told the officer, "Nobody there is in any shape to drive."

"You're telling me that out of all those people there, not one person is sober enough to drive?" the officer asked, shocked.

"Umm . . . yes," I said, thinking it shouldn't be too surprising.

"Jesus Christ." The officer shook his head in dismay.

Since nobody could come get me, one officer drove me home in my van while the other followed behind. I thanked them for their leniency as they drove away, but it felt bittersweet. I had been sober on my way to pick up a drunk friend—I was honestly being responsible. Sadly, I did a lot of drunk driving back then, but this was the one time I really wasn't the slightest bit impaired.

A few days later, my lawyer, John, called to inform me of a settlement offer for my lawsuit over my accident. The insurance company was offering me sixty thousand dollars—basically, what it would cost them to fight my lawyer in court. John suggested I accept the offer, which I did. Obviously, I wanted more, but I knew I had no case. I was the dumbass drunk who dove into two inches of water, so I had nobody else to blame, at least not in a legal sense.

I also told John about my DUI, and he said he'd get his partner, Chris, a criminal defense lawyer, to help me with that. He reassured me Chris was a shark, and considering I was at the legal limit, I'd get off with a slap on the wrist. I felt a little better about that situation and was ecstatic about the thought of getting forty thousand dollars after John got a third of the sixty thousand I had won.

What I didn't know was the state was also entitled to a third of that settlement because they had covered medical bills related to my injury and disability. It sucked, but there wasn't shit I could do. I even visited my legislator to complain, but he just said sorry. After paying off my credit cards, I ended up with about seven thousand dollars, which I just decided to blow on strippers, booze, and cocaine.

Part of the problem was I couldn't stand living at home with my parents, and I hated not having true independence. Don't get me wrong—I appreciated everything my parents did for me, especially my mother. Even though my sister was my PCA, my mom was my primary caregiver. Still, I wanted my own place like any normal person in their twenties, and living with Mom and Dad doesn't bold well for one's dating life.

I thought I'd be able to possibly buy a house with the settlement money, but those dreams were shattered. Now I was stuck at home without my driver's license, which I had lost with my DUI, constantly battling bowel and bladder issues. Obstacles perpetually mounted no matter what I did, so I decided to party like a rock star and forget about all the depressing shit going on.

For the next couple of months, I went on a rampage with a no-fucks-given attitude. I even started driving on a suspended license. Eventually, I got caught, which further complicated my DUI, but Chris miraculously got my charges reduced to careless driving, and I only got two years' probation. He even got my license reinstated, so it literally felt like there were zero repercussions from my bad decision.

Now I had simply the wrong type of empowerment. I was always driving everybody around in the Disco Dodge, which is what my friends called my van because it was a virtual nightclub on wheels. We'd pack that thing full of people and start drinking, doing drugs, blasting music, and bar-hopping across town. Looking back, I can't believe how stupid and careless that was.

That type of arrogance only spells trouble. A pimped-out, pearl-white minivan parked outside all the different bars at night is something the police are going to eventually notice. I even got pulled over a couple times drunk and they let me off with a clear warning to stop fucking around. The police put me on notice. I didn't care, though—I was pissed off at life. To me it was innocent partying and fun.

I even tried driving to Perkins completely inebriated on my birthday, of all nights. I made it about a mile before the flashing red lights lit up my rearview mirror. I was so wasted I didn't even bother the officer with all the formalities. I just rolled down the window and told him to take me to jail. I knew I wasn't getting out of this one. The smell of alcohol emanating from my van was enough to fail a breathalyzer.

At the jail, I refused all the tests and demanded my phone call. I called John at four in the morning, and a couple of hours later, I was released. Chris managed to prevent my license from getting suspended, and a couple of days after that, I got my van out of impound despite the state's efforts to confiscate it outright. The two of them were brilliant attorneys, legal Picassos. I felt invincible.

I knew John and Chris were getting concerned about my behavior, but I was sure that as lawyers, they'd seen a lot of shit. Still, they cared about me and knew I was battling some demons. They were more than just my attorneys—I was becoming good friends with them as well. I sought out John's advice on numerous matters. He was so pragmatic and offered me more guidance then any counselor, psychologist, or clergy that I consulted with.

Besides, all my friends were getting DUIs at that time, and I was sending so much business to John and Chris it was hard for them to stay mad. I became their cash cow, so I got preferential treatment. Even though Chris and John lectured me all the time, I was still their client, along with dozens of my friends. I knew they were going to have my back regardless of the stupid shit I continued to do.

Of course, my behavior wasn't doing anything conducive for my living situation at home, and there was definitely increased tension between my parents and me. I could sense my mother and father weren't in a happy marriage. The day I came home from the hospital, I knew we were not a happy family. Their relationship was already fragile, and my accident was the straw that broke the camel's back.

One early morning, as I lay in bed still sleeping, my dad came into my room and told me goodbye before heading off to work. He did this every so often, but I did find it strange that on this morning he was dressed in jeans and a flannel instead of a suit. After he left, I didn't think anything else of it because, as a salesman, he could get away with stuff like that.

It was my day off, and I couldn't go anywhere with my driver's license suspended, so I just lounged around the house all day waiting for my parents to get home. It was probably around 7 p.m. when my mom finally got home after staying a couple of hours late at work.

She asked me where my father was, and I told her he hadn't come home from work yet. She headed to her bedroom to change out of her work clothes, and after about ten minutes, she came back out crying. She was holding a letter in her hand.

"Your dad left," she cried.

"What do you mean, 'He left'?" I asked, confused.

"He's gone, left! These are divorce papers and a farewell letter."

After twenty-eight years of marriage, my dad had finally had enough and decided to divorce my mother. He hired a lawyer to draft up papers leaving my mom both houses they owned together as well as the majority of their retirement account. The only things my dad took were a few thousand dollars cash and our dog, Tasha, who I only then realized had been out of sight all day.

I learned later that my dad had driven to upstate New York, where he tried to cross the border into Canada so he could live in the woods right off the land. Since he couldn't get across the border, he stayed in New York, where he built a shelter within the side of a hill. He fished, hunted, and escaped the rat race to be one with nature.

My dad was an avid outdoorsman, and this was his dream. I guess he finally got sick of the mundane nine-to-five sales job and the way my mom always bitched at him to get things done around the house. This was his way of leaving in the least contentious way he knew how. Communication was never my father's greatest attribute, and I guess he didn't want any conflict or criticism.

I guess he could have handled the situation in a more mature manner, but I can't blame him for leaving the way he did. My dad didn't want to argue and talk things through, nor did he want any-body telling him what he was planning was crazy. Some family members accused him of abandoning me, but I didn't see it that way and actually defended his choice.

My dad was a Vietnam vet who had witnessed his best friend getting blown to pieces right next to him. I heard the nightmares and I read the poems—my dad had unresolved issues from his time fighting in a shitty war and wasn't happy with his job or marriage. I also know my accident impacted him greatly. He felt terrible about what had happened to me and didn't know how to cope with all these issues plaguing his life.

He escaped to the wilderness like I escaped to the bar, and that's how we dealt with our problems and depression. I wasn't mad at him for leaving, nor was I going to miss him. I wanted nothing but for him to find peace, happiness, and contentment, just like I was seeking. I also knew he wasn't gone forever. My dad loved and cared about me, and he'd be back when the time was right.

As long as I had my mother, I knew I'd be safe. I preferred her doing my cares anyway. The connection I had with her had only grown stronger every day since I broke my neck. Like a mother cares for her cubs in the wild, my mother cared for me. She was my guardian angel and would never abandon me, despite my reckless disregard for life at that time.

My mother was devastated after my father left. Not only did divorce conflict with her religious beliefs, I felt there were some unresolved issues that she had that could never be worked out now. However, my mom deserved better, and my dad deserved happiness, too. They hadn't even been sleeping in the same bed or having fun together anymore. Sometimes, couples stay together for too long for the wrong reasons, and I believe this was one of those situations. I was putting myself in both of my parents' shoes, and I guess that's why I wasn't as upset about their divorce as my mother was.

My mother may not have recognized it then, but I believe my dad did her a huge favor. I think she would have preferred to try to make their marriage work, but personally, I thought this was the best thing that could have happened for the two of them. That divorce was a blessing in disguise; I just knew it would take my mom a couple of years to realize it.

Unfortunately, she now was responsible for two mortgages, and we went from a two-income household down to one income. I wasn't working and most of my disability went toward my van payment, gas, and insurance. The stress of taking care of all the bills along with a handicapped son was taking a toll on my mother physically and mentally.

I was surprised how well she handled everything and kept it together like superglue. Even so, it was difficult. My mother tried not to show emotion, but I could see it in her body language and heard the cries from her room at night. I should have been more supportive, but I honestly believed her problems paled in comparison to mine. I was selfish and felt self-entitled because of my disability. When I wasn't trying to numb my own pain with drugs and alcohol, mentally I just tried to block out everything else going on in my life.

CHAPTER EIGHTEEN

◆ ◆ ◆ ◆ ◆ ◆ ◆ ◆ ◆

Rebel Without a Cause

E VEN THOUGH IT HAD BEEN over three years since my accident, I was still having trouble accepting my new life as a quadriplegic. It didn't matter how much I tried concentrating on the positive aspects of my life—the negative attributes of a spinal cord injury reign supreme. I couldn't escape them, no matter how hard I tried. Subsequently, my downfall continued.

It helped having great attorneys to help navigate life's pitfalls, and at this point in my life, my lawyers were my saving grace. The case for my DUI got dragged out for quite some time, but when my day in court finally did arrive, the situation turned rather tense. I knew I was potentially facing some time in jail. What I didn't expect was deputies waiting for me to arrive so they could slap cuffs on me and haul me away.

Unbeknownst to my lawyer, a warrant had been issued for my arrest because I violated my probation by getting a second DUI. I also got caught driving on a revoked license a couple of months before my court date. To make matters worse, I refused a breathalyzer—another crime—with my DUI. I was scared shitless about getting locked up. Chris was good, but I had so much shit hanging over me. I thought I was fucked for sure.

A flurry of activity and negotiations ensued, with Chris running in and out of the judge's chambers. The entire time, two deputies stood right behind me with their handcuffs ready, patiently waiting like disciplined soldiers for their orders.

After what seemed like an hour, Chris finally came hustling over to me with beads of sweat running down his forehead. He sat down next to me and began to explain why the warrant had been issued and how he got the judge to squash it. He also had a plea deal that he strongly recommended I take: thirty days of house arrest, three years of probation, and a $200 fine.

"No jail time?" I asked, surprised.

"Nope," Chris replied. "That prosecutor was being a real prick, but you had a cool judge. Don't fuck up now, OK, Eric?" Chris demanded. "No more drinking and driving."

Considering my charges and the jail time I was potentially facing, I couldn't have been more pleased with how that case turned out. However, now I was an official ward of the state, as I liked to refer to it. Every aspect of my life was about to be scrutinized by my probation officer and other bureaucrats within the criminal justice system. There were strict guidelines to my plea bargain that I had to agree to, and zero tolerance for my continued mischief.

I agreed to start my house arrest two weeks from my court date. In the meantime, I had to meet with my probation officer, who was named after a sandwich, but I'll just call him Grumpy. He was old, cranky, and had no sense of humor. He told me I would need to have an alcohol assessment as ordered by the courts and must follow the recommendation of that assessment. Grumpy also said I would be subjected to random drug testing and, as ordered by the judge, must abstain from alcohol completely.

A week after meeting with Grumpy, the day came for me to turn myself in for house arrest. I was nervous as hell that day because I had to go to the workhouse to get processed, and that place was like a prison complex. I was feeling unusually anxious even though I knew I would be getting released the same day, so I decided to smoke just a little marijuana beforehand to help calm my nerves.

My sister dropped me off at the razor-wired gates of hell, and when I wheeled inside, it was everything I suspected. I had to sit in this shitty, smelly, musty holding area with other degenerates like myself waiting to get processed. There was one toilet for twenty people to share, and one by one, we all waited patiently for our names to be called. After a couple of hours went by, a guard finally came back and got me.

He led me through some doors and into a changing room, where he asked me if I needed help getting out of my clothes. Immediately, my heart sank into my stomach, and I told him emphatically that I was here to get processed for house arrest, not jail! The guard explained that it didn't matter. I would have to go through the same procedures as a regular inmate whether I was there for house arrest or jail time.

The guards helped me change into my prison scrubs and then led me through the long corridors, past general population, and—thankfully—into the medical ward. The medical ward was a separate unit of the workhouse that resembled a small ward at a hospital with real beds, a television, and an accessible bathroom and shower. Plus, there was only one other inmate I had to share the place with. Despite its comforts, though, I had no interest in staying any longer than I had to.

Shortly after arriving at the medical ward, another guard returned with some paperwork for me to sign and then handed me a cup to pee in for my drug test. I was confused and questioned why I needed to take a drug test. The guard explained that in order to get released for house arrest, I must pass a drug test first. Now my heart really sank because I knew I was fucked this time. I had just smoked a joint two hours prior.

It made sense, though. The judge had ordered me to abstain from alcohol and drugs, and now the state was making sure I was abiding by my plea agreement. This was the type of shit that went in one ear and out the other, though. I didn't care what the judge said. I had great lawyers. I had a disability. I made my own rules. If I wanted to smoke marijuana before getting processed for house arrest, then I should be able to—it was just a little weed! This was my constant frame of mind.

Of course, I failed the drug test. The guard informed me I could take it again tomorrow, but if I failed that one, it would be three days before I could take a drug test again. After that, it would be a week, then two weeks, and so on. I knew marijuana can stay in your system up to a month, so I was in a state of sheer panic. I desperately tried to get in touch with my lawyers, which is difficult to do from a prison telephone. At that point, I thought I was going to be trapped inside this Russian gulag for a month.

As the day progressed, I got to know more about my fellow inmate, Julius, who had burns all over his body from setting his girlfriend's car on fire. From talking with him, it sounded like it was a serious domestic situation, and he was looking at some significant jail time. Julius was very apologetic, though, and from what he described, he had a difficult life on top of his relationship issues. To make matters worse, the girlfriend's son had beaten him up with a baseball bat. He was busted up.

The two of us talked all day and into the night. I told him the story of how I ended up paralyzed and the difficulties I had adjusting to life in a wheelchair. We talked about our favorite movies and our love for hip-hop music, and then I started rapping the lyrics to my favorite Tupac and Snoop Dogg songs.

Julius couldn't believe I knew the songs verbatim and started beatboxing as I rapped the lyrics. I could tell my companionship was lifting his spirits, but I made clear to Julius my desire to get out of there as quickly as possible. I was thankful to be there alone with him instead of in general population, though, because jail is no place for a young, good-looking, completely vulnerable guy like me.

When I tried to sleep that night, the place sounded like an insane asylum. People were constantly screaming, and their echoes filled up the entire prison. It was impossible to sleep, and I was dreading the thought of having to be there another night—or longer.

In the morning, Julius came over and handed me a urinal filled with his piss, telling me it was for my drug test. I was a little surprised by his willingness to help me, and then I asked him if he was able to pass a drug test.

Julius said, "Hell, yeah! I ain't no druggie!" We both started to laugh.

"Julius, if this works, I will come back and put money in your account for commissary," I told him.

"I would really appreciate that, Eric," he replied excitedly.

Later that morning, a guard came into the medical ward to administer my second drug test, so I handed him the urinal filled with Julius's piss. He then told me that typically, they have to watch me urinate, but I explained to him that because of my disability and the fact that I use a catheter, I was on a schedule and couldn't just pee at will. The guard stood there looking at me perplexed, so I lifted my shirt and showed him how I catheterize through my belly button. Thankfully, that seemed to convince him.

A couple of hours later, the guard returned with some paperwork for me to sign and told me I passed the test. I tried not to look surprised or happy, but once he left the ward, Julius and I started celebrating. I sang, he danced around, and then we gave each other high-fives.

Julius was a black guy raised on the inner-city streets of Chicago. I was a white kid from an upper middle-class suburb in Minnesota, yet we had a unique connection—bonded by the hardships of life. It almost felt like we were breaking out of prison together, only he had sacrificed his freedom for mine. We both had a mutual respect for one another that crossed any racial disparities.

I thanked Julius for what he had done, essentially giving me freedom. I told him I was a man of my word and to check his jail account in a couple of days. I could tell he was sad I was leaving but happy that he was going to have some money to buy some much-needed items from the commissary. The following day, I had my sister drive to the jail and deposit money in Julius's account. I kept my word and hoped for the best for him.

Over the next thirty days of house arrest, I did everything I was told to do—even abstaining from all drugs and alcohol. I wasn't taking any risks with all the jail time hanging over my head. After almost being stuck in the workhouse for a month, I was scared straight. It only took one night in jail for me to realize I never wanted to go back there.

I kept myself busy with work, picking up a couple extra speaking engagements on my days off from the bank. I did feel a little guilty, though, because some of those speeches were to a few driver education classes, and there were people from Mothers Against Drunk Drivers (MADD) speaking as well. I'd finish up my speech, and the MADD representative would come out into the hallway and tell me how powerful of a speech I had given and praise me for my advocacy. Little did they know I was wearing an ankle bracelet from a DUI offense. Sometimes I felt like a complete piece of shit, but other times I couldn't help but giggle at the irony.

That pretty much epitomized the conflict of interest I had going on. I kept speaking about the dangers of making poor decisions while using drugs or alcohol, and then I'd go out and make poor decisions after a night of partying with drugs and alcohol. Do as I say, not as I do, I told myself repeatedly. That's how I justified my hypocrisy.

I knew my message to all those students was the right one. Furthermore, I could tell that not only could those kids relate to me, I was also making a difference. It didn't matter to me that I was a hypocrite. Ultimately, I thought, the ends justified the means. What they didn't know didn't hurt them. Besides, I was a sincere, heartfelt, passionate messenger. To me, that's what mattered the most: the message, not whether I practiced what I preached.

At the time, I even had a couple stories written about me regarding my accident and public speaking, not only in our local paper but also in one of the two major newspapers in our entire state. It was a feel-good story about defying the odds and over-coming adversity. The articles played up how I was such an inspiration, but of course, I was never honest about my drug or alcohol use during the interviews.

I wasn't looking for fame—the reporters found me. For the most part, I was upfront with them about everything we talked about. I told them it was still hard accepting my disability and forgetting my past life, but ultimately, the stories made it sound like everything was just fucking peachy in my life. They portrayed a young kid struck by tragedy, overcoming obstacles to inspire other young kids. It was all bullshit, though.

The farce continued once I completed my house arrest and was free of the electronic monitoring device around my ankle. I started drinking and doing blow again. It didn't even matter to me that I was on probation or that I had to complete a treatment program because of my chemical assessment. I went about my days and nights as if I had never even been arrested and pled guilty to my DUI—smoking weed, going to the bars, and doing cocaine.

I had to meet with my probation officer, Grumpy, once a month. Even though he always breathalyzed me when I got there, he never really hassled me if I was going to my treatment sessions and had my AA signatures, which I always forged. One day, though, he dropped a bombshell on me and handed me a slip with an address on it, telling me I needed to go there for a drug test within twenty-four hours. That was a first for him. Grumpy had told me I would be subject to random UAs, but again, I hadn't listened.

There was no getting out of this test either. I used every medical excuse I had in my playbook, but Grumpy knew I still had to urinate, so he told me to get it done! Knowing I was going to fail and thinking about the ramifications of another probation violation, I knew I needed to come up with an idea to pass this drug test, or I was fucked.

Desperate times call for desperate situations, so I needed a plan, and quick. I remembered a movie I had watched a couple of weeks prior about college football. In the movie, there was a scene where a player on steroids needed to pass a drug test, so a medical student used a catheter to inject clean urine into his bladder right before the test. It was basically the same thing I had to do when I did my bladder flushes with sterile water, so I figured I could do the same thing with somebody else's urine.

This was typical of the crazy antics that accompanied my rebellious attitude at the time, and I thought it was a brilliant idea. I already had all the necessary medical tools to pull it off: syringes, catheters, and sterilizers. All I needed was some clean urine, which actually wasn't a problem to find. Despite all of my friends who did drugs, I also had a bunch who just drank beer, so it wouldn't be difficult finding somebody to donate some clean urine for me.

The next morning, I stopped by a sober friend's apartment and grabbed some piss from him, and then drove to the drug testing facility and made my way to the first-floor public bathroom. I went into a stall and took out all my supplies, which I had brought in with a small bag. I drained my bladder first and then injected my friend's clean urine inside me. This wasn't mad science—all it took was a catheter and a large syringe. Afterwards, I went upstairs to the floor where the drug testing was administered and took a number. Ten minutes later, an old guy escorted me to a private bathroom, watched me catheterize myself and pee into a cup, and then showed me the exit.

A week later, I got a call from Grumpy informing me I had passed. My plan had worked perfectly, and I felt like I had just discovered the secret to clean, sustainable energy. I could do it again any time Grumpy ordered a drug test, so it was a virtual green light to do whatever I wanted despite my probation restrictions. It was clearly a foolproof plan.

Through all my insubordination, my mother was there supporting me physically, emotionally, and financially. She didn't know the true extent of my insurrection, though—if she had, I doubt she would have been so helpful. I was very selfish during that stage in my life, and in retrospect, I feel bad for taking advantage of my mother's unconditional love and empathy for her child. I needed her for every aspect of my life, though, so I thought I had no choice but to constantly lie.

My mom was still acting as my primary caregiver, never hesitating to clean up the bowel accidents I was causing with my perpetual drug use. She cooked, paid the bills, and sometimes worked two jobs trying to keep us afloat. I should have been more understanding and respectful, but I believed my problems took precedence over hers. Most of the time, though, I just didn't think about it at all. I was becoming numb to life in general.

When she met a new guy at her new job, it was such a relief. They started going out on dates, and my mother would come home with a glow about her I hadn't seen in years. This new guy was a gentleman and very hardworking; furthermore, he had lost both his sons when they were fairly young, so he and my mom had a similar connection with tragedies in their lives.

The two of them were falling in love, and eventually, he asked my mom to move in with him. She said yes, of course, and I couldn't have been more excited. My mom was a saint and deserved true happiness—not to mention I would have the house to myself. She told me I could rent it from her and get a roommate for the basement to split the cost.

I had pretty much done what I wanted while I was living with my parents, but now, with zero parental supervision, my defiance of rules and norms really went to a whole new level. I started driving my van again with a revoked license, and I eventually got caught a couple of times. This was a clear violation of the rules of my probation, which required me to abide by the law, but I never even thought about the ramifications of my actions. I had great legal representation, creative ways to pass drug tests, and unlimited excuses. I felt untouchable.

Because my lawyers were always helping me out and were such skilled attorneys, I thought I could completely flaunt the law. My thought process was irrational and upside down. I felt entitled to screw off, drink, drive, hustle, and scam—whatever it took to make it through my shitty life. Chris and John couldn't keep me out of trouble forever, though, and inevitably, my actions would soon have consequences that I couldn't cleverly avoid.

CHAPTER NINETEEN

◆ ◆ ◆ ◆ ◆ ◆ ◆ ◆ ◆

Jailbird

I WAS RELAXING AT HOME one evening when I heard a loud banging on my front door. Immediately, I became concerned. Nobody I knew would knock on my front door because I couldn't do the steps. The pounding continued, so I wheeled into the spare bedroom to peek out the window and see who it was. What I saw were two squad cars and about a half-dozen police officers with flashlights in hand. I knew this wasn't good, so I wheeled into my bathroom, locked the door, and called my lawyer.

My lawyer told me to stay inside my house until he could make some phone calls in the morning to find out what was going on. I assured him I had no plans of leaving my bathroom, let alone my house, and I would be anxiously awaiting his call the next day. After about twenty minutes or so I came out of the bathroom and saw that the police had finally left.

John called me the morning after and told me that since I was caught driving with a revoked license, I had violated my probation, and now there was a warrant for my arrest. The rules of my probation were cut and dried: I must remain a law-abiding citizen. That term had always seemed so vague to me, though. Jaywalking, running a stop sign, and even lying to certain people could be considered against the law, and in my eyes, people broke the law every day. Because of that, I never took my probation that seriously.

John informed me that getting caught driving with a revoked license clearly crossed the line and was considered a criminal act.

Now I had to go through the whole arrest and court process all over again. He told me to rest easy, though, because he had made arrangements for me to turn myself in for booking, and I would be released right afterwards.

A couple of days later, that's exactly what happened. I turned myself in to the police station, got fingerprinted, had my mugshot taken, and then was released on my own recognizance. Then, a couple of nights after that, the cops were pounding at my front door again. It turns out I had another warrant issued for another probation violation—the second driving after revocation—so the cat and mouse game between myself and the police began again.

I told my roommate not to answer the front door while I continued to lay low, locked away in my bedroom. I couldn't reach my lawyers because they were out of town or in court, so all I could do was hide. Those were stressful days, and I was beginning to regret thumbing my nose at the law on so many occasions. What would be next? I imagined wanted posters with my picture posted around the streets of White Bear Lake.

As I was getting dropped off after work one afternoon, there were several police officers waiting for me in my driveway. I knew why they were there and immediately started begging and pleading with them not to take me away. I explained to them I knew I had a warrant, and that my lawyer had arranged for me to turn myself in. I promised that's exactly what I planned to do in the morning. They were nice enough not to take me to jail, but they warned me they'd be back the next day if I didn't turn myself in.

At that point, I had grown all too familiar with the practice of getting booked, processed, and released. Because of this and the fact I always had solid legal representation, I began to get complacent. I decided to call my attorney in the morning before I went down to the police station, but when I couldn't get in touch with him, I had no choice but to turn myself in alone. I was a little nervous about doing that, but I had always been released before, so I assumed the same thing would happen this time.

Sadly, I assumed wrong. After taking my mugshot and finger-prints, the guards put me in a holding cell with several other individuals. I was then informed I was being transferred to the Adult Detention Center (ADC).

The ADC was an underground facility built into the bluff along the Mississippi River in St. Paul. It was old and dingy, and it looked like a North Korean prison camp. Once I arrived, I grew extremely anxious because I could tell this was no place for a quadriplegic. Having to take an elevator underground to reach the jail was scary in itself. As I was slowly lowered below the streets of St. Paul, the sunlight dissipated, taking with it my freedom, liberty, and privileges.

The guards escorted me to a room where they helped me change into bright orange prison attire. The jail suit was old and torn to pieces, and I began to get nervous about my situation. I asked the guards repeatedly how long I was going to be held for, and they told me that would be determined by a judge. I articulated all my medical needs, hoping this would somehow expedite my time there, but the guards really didn't seem to give a shit.

I was taken to the medical ward of the ADC, which really wasn't a medical ward. It was simply a separate unit of the jail facility that housed inmates with medical issues. There were no hospital beds or accessible bathrooms like the workhouse I had been to. In fact, I couldn't even access the toilets. The food was horrendous, and there were several other inmates packed into a small area. These guys were the only positive part of my situation. They were hardened criminals but surprisingly sympathetic to my disability, and they were all very helpful.

That experience was definitely a reality check. I may have thought I could disregard the terms of my probation but sitting in my jail cell at the ADC was a tough reminder that I wasn't above the law. I was no longer a free citizen. I was once again a ward of the state, and there was nothing I could do about it but sit and wait. I had plenty of time to think about my predicament and how I had gotten myself into this big mess. That was the purpose of jail and isolation from society, I reckoned.

I hated that place with a passion. There was a phone in our unit for inmates to use, but it was tucked behind a steel table welded to the jailhouse floor. Luckily, my fellow inmates helped me onto the bench so I could gain access to it. I tried calling my lawyers, but unfortunately couldn't reach either John or Chris. With no other options, all I could do was bide my time until morning when I would get to plead my case to a judge.

As nighttime approached, a guard came to our unit and dispensed medications to all my fellow inmates. I wasn't surprised my prescriptions weren't included, but I also knew the jail was required by law to provide me with my necessary meds. I asked the guard where my medication was, and of course he didn't know. I made sure to communicate the importance of my prescriptions for my various medical conditions.

Trying to sleep at the ADC was akin to torture. Getting any rest on a thin mat on top of a concrete slab is nearly impossible when you have a disability such as mine. Add in all the snoring, yelling, and cold, dry air being pumped throughout the ventilation, and it made for a long, miserable night. At least I had all night to think about what I would say to the judge in the morning, including a complaint about the inaccessible conditions I was being held in. I rehearsed my speech over and over like I was about to make my case to the U.S. Supreme Court.

The following day, guards started to come to our unit early in the morning and remove inmates who had court hearings. I waited patiently for them to come get me, but morning soon turned to afternoon, and I had still not been called upon. I asked a guard what was going on with my hearing, and he just told me it was probably later in the day. However, when the second group of inmates was removed for afternoon court proceedings, I was left to stew in my own anxiety.

I knew at that point I was fucked because it was a Friday, and I certainly wasn't seeing a judge on Saturday. I was in full-blown panic mode and made numerous desperate and unsuccessful attempts to contact my attorneys. I called my mother next and told her about my situation, and she told me that she would bring my medications down to the jail. That brought me temporary relief—at least I wouldn't have to suffer through another night without my meds.

My relief was short-lived. Later that evening, the guard came to our unit to dole out the daily medications, and once again, mine were not included. I informed the guard that I hadn't gotten my meds the night before and that my mom should have brought my prescriptions down to the jail. The guard told me he'd go check. When he returned a few minutes later, he informed me my medication had been taken over to the workhouse because I was going to be transferred there.

However, I was never transferred to the workhouse that weekend, nor was I given any of my medications. Furthermore, I was going through heavy withdrawals from not having access to the prescription drugs that I'd been taking since my accident. I was in a significant amount of pain, suffering from severe muscle spasms, and using the same dirty catheter that I had brought with me when I turned myself in several days earlier.

I was also still unable to get in touch with my lawyers. When I complained, the guards didn't seem to care. My mother was doing her best to help, but she was getting the runaround from everybody she spoke with over the phone.

I'm in favor of being held accountable for my actions, and I also believe in karma, but my treatment at ADC was undeserved. I had a severe disability, and I didn't need my attorneys to tell me that withholding much-needed medications was a gross violation of my civil rights. I knew what their obligations were at the jail, and I knew what my rights were. I was suffering at that point, abut there was nothing I could do.

Finally, on Monday morning, a guard came to my cell to get me and take me to my court hearing. I was relieved but extremely aggravated, and I made sure anyone wearing a uniform and badge knew about it along my way.

As I wheeled through the long underground corridors, I could also tell my treatment at the facility was messing with my brain. I was light-headed and dizzy, and I even noticed my vision was blurry. I had to stop frequently along the way to gather my composure, but the guards showed zero compassion for my predicament.

After waiting in a holding cell for a couple of hours, I got to talk with a public defender. I was escorted into a small room with bright lights, where I listened to a young Asian woman read off a host of offenses I was being charged with. I was confused because I knew that I violated my probation by driving without a license, but the public defender listed off other charges as well, offenses I had never even heard of before.

We were only able to converse for a few short minutes before being whisked away into the courtroom to face the judge. Inside, the scene turned rather chaotic. The prosecutor started talking, then the public defender, and their voices were echoing throughout the courtroom. The court proceedings seemed far too serious for somebody accused of driving without a license.

The judge started asking me questions that I was having difficulty comprehending. I was still somewhat dizzy from going without my medications for so long. I tried to explain that I did not recognize the charges against me, nor did I want the public defender representing me. When the judge asked me to elaborate, I emphatically stated that I had an attorney defending me but was unable to get in contact with him.

The judge clearly didn't like the fact that I was there without my lawyer, so he continued my case and set a different date for my court proceedings. I was escorted back to the ADC, where I was placed in another holding area and told I was going to be transferred to the workhouse shortly. I was rather upset my hearing in front of the judge didn't go exactly as planned, but I was relieved I would finally be getting out of the ADC to a place where I could get my prescriptions and proper medical care. I wasn't getting released but getting out of the ADC was enough consolation at that stage.

As the day progressed, inmates were removed from the holding cell one by one and placed into vans for transport. I waited patiently for my turn, but the end of the workday approached quickly, and I found myself all alone in the holding area. I began to ask the guards when I was going to be transferred to the workhouse, but they all gave me the runaround.

Finally, a young guard came into the holding area and said, "I'm sorry, Eric, but we can't transfer you to the workhouse."

"Why not?" I asked, disturbed.

"The warden told us they just repaved the parking lot there, so we can't get you into the entrance."

"Why the hell not? How are the other inmates getting in?"

"There's another entrance, but it has stairs," the guard explained. "Me and a couple of the other guys offered to carry you up the stairs, but they still said no."

"That's where my medication is, though," I insisted. "They told my mom to take my prescriptions there because that's where I was being transferred."

"I'm sorry. Personally, I think it's bullshit," the guard told me. "It's only a few steps—I know we can get you up them no problem."

"I need my fucking meds!" I exclaimed.

"I realize that," the guard said caringly. "Me and the other guys feel bad. I'll make sure the county nurse comes to talk to you before they send you back up to your cell, OK?" The guard put his hand on my shoulder and apologized again as I started to cry tears of sheer terror at the thought of going back upstairs. The kind guard could clearly see I was distressed, so he assured me again that he would get the nurse to talk to me right away.

When the nurse arrived she seemed disinterested in my situation. She asked me several questions regarding my disability and medical needs, and vaguely said she'd see what she could do about my meds. Distraught, I sat crying in that holding cage for another hour or so before a guard escorted me back to my cold, dingy jail cell in the medical ward. There he gave me the nastiest bologna sandwich for dinner. It was food not even fit for rats to eat.

Later that evening, when the other inmates received their medications, mine were missing once again. I was livid and, at this point, completely distressed. I begged and pleaded with the guard to get me my medication and reiterated the conversation I had with the nurse earlier that evening. The guard told me he would go check, but when he returned a few minutes later, he still didn't have my meds. I couldn't believe what was occurring, but I knew right then I had to take matters into my own hands.

There was no way I could spend another night at the ADC. Obviously, nobody was taking my medical needs seriously, so desperate times called for desperate measures. I needed to get out of there as quickly as possible but escaping from jail was out of the question. I couldn't propel down any walls with a rope made from bedsheets, and I certainly couldn't tunnel my way out with a plastic spoon. The only way I could get myself out of there was faking some medical emergency or pretending to try to commit suicide.

I wheeled around the medical ward looking for cameras and checked to see if any guards could see into my jail cell. After determining nobody could see me, I made my move. I wheeled over to the window in the corner of my cell and took a bunch of deep breaths, pounding my chest to hype myself up for what I was about to do.

With everybody in their beds and nobody watching, I repeatedly bashed my head into the brick wall as hard as I could bear. I did this several times until I felt the warm blood dripping down my face. After I was satisfied with the size of the cut on my forehead, I wheeled toward my bed and threw myself out of my wheelchair. Once I was on the floor I screamed as loudly as I could in agony and pain.

"Ahhhhh, somebody help!" I yelled. "Help me, please!"

After a few minutes, one of my fellow inmates came running into my cell, and after noticing all the blood, he went to retrieve a guard on duty in our unit. A couple of guards rushed in and assessed the situation, and after noticing all the blood, they called for the paramedics. Several minutes later, the paramedics arrived and transported me to the hospital on a stretcher.

They asked me what had happened, and I told them I was having severe muscle spasms that caused me to fall out of my chair and hit my head. I wasn't being entirely truthful, but I didn't care. I was on my way to the hospital and out of the ADC, and that's all that mattered. Now the only thing I needed to worry about was whether they would send me back there after taking me to the hospital.

Once I arrived at the hospital, doctors ran some tests and took X-rays of my head and neck. The whole time I was there, I was extremely embarrassed. I was handcuffed to my hospital bed, still wearing the bright orange jumpsuit from the ADC. These were doctors and nurses I knew from my time at the hospital after my accident, and I kept explaining to them all how this was a very big misunderstanding.

Fortunately for me, the plan worked. After several hours at the hospital, I was informed by the guard watching over me that I was going to be transferred to the workhouse instead of back to the ADC. Apparently, upper management had finally come to the realization that the facility wasn't adequately equipped to meet my medical needs.

Coincidentally, the freshly repaved parking lot at the workhouse was no longer an obstruction. I was relieved but infuriated nonetheless. The substandard treatment and care I received while being held at the ADC were unacceptable. It was about time I got to leave that hellhole.

I arrived at the workhouse late that evening after the nursing staff had already left, so there was nothing I could do but go straight to bed. I was exhausted anyway, mentally and physically drained from everything I had gone through over the past five days, which seemed like an eternity at this point.

In the morning, the nurse came in to give me my meds, but she would only give me one day's worth. I told her I was five days behind and going through withdrawals, but she didn't seem to care. I tried to explain that my medication worked by building up in my bloodstream, so a single dose would not return me to the levels needed to relieve my pain and spasms. I needed a higher dose to relieve my symptoms. Still, she didn't care, and I only received one dose.

After taking my prescriptions, I went over to the phone and tried calling my lawyer again. Thankfully, I was finally able to get in touch with John. I told him about my whole ordeal with a desperation in my voice that I had never used with him before. He was angry and sympathetic, and immediately went to work securing my release.

It didn't take him long, either. Later that afternoon, a couple of guards came into the medical ward and told me I was free to go. A wave of relief rushed through my body. I called my mother to come pick me up, and as I wheeled outside through those razor-wired fences, the sun, warm breeze, and refreshing sense of freedom had never felt so good. It felt almost as good as if somebody had cured my paralysis.

John stopped over later that evening to talk about my tribulation over the last week. I explained everything that occurred—the withholding of my prescriptions, my mom bringing down my meds, the false charges, the bullshit about the repaved parking lot—the whole works.

"Why the fuck didn't you call me before turning yourself in?" John exclaimed.

"I did. I couldn't get in touch with you or Chris," I replied.

"Yeah, Chris was up north for court, and I was on vacation," John explained. "Still, our secretary should have forwarded us the messages."

"Now what?" I asked.

"Now we're going to sue those motherfuckers!" John said angrily. "They can't treat people like that, especially people in your condition."

John explained to me how my treatment was negligence and a gross violation of my civil rights. I was entitled to my prescriptions, access to a bathroom, nurses, and the like. The fact that they had told my mother to take my medications elsewhere and then never took me there made them all the more liable. This was all music to my ears.

Not only was I starting to see dollar signs, I wanted revenge— maybe not necessarily revenge, but accountability. I surely wasn't the only guy in a wheelchair with legal issues, and both John and I wanted to be certain nobody had to experience what I did ever again. We weren't simply going to let this matter go. I didn't just want compensation for pain and suffering. I wanted a change in policy and procedures.

CHAPTER TWENTY

◆ ◆ ◆ ◆ ◆ ◆ ◆ ◆ ◆

Summer of Love

ONE WOULD THINK THAT SUCH an agonizing time spent in jail would set somebody like me straight, but unfortunately, it had the exact opposite effect. I was pissed off at the system, and after John told me he was filing a lawsuit against the county, I became even more combative. I was growing increasingly agitated with my whole situation, and for the first time in my life, I started to experience constant symptoms of severe anxiety and insomnia.

I made an appointment with my doctor, and he started prescribing me Valium. At first the drug worked wonders. Not only did it relax me and help me sleep at night, but it also got rid of my muscle spasms. Better yet, the Valium made me forget about all my problems. I'd forget about the constant nerve pain I dealt with daily and about the loss of my perfect life. Furthermore, the valium was incredibly effective at completely alleviating the crashes of a night of partying with cocaine, as I discovered accidentally.

I went through the motions for a couple of months as I waited anxiously for my license to be reinstated, but a couple of months after getting my license back, I fucked up again. All the drugs and alcohol I was consuming just numbed my senses, most notably common sense. One night as I was driving a group of people home from a club, I got pulled over again and charged with another DUI.

This third DUI was no joke, either. I had really put myself in a precarious situation. The state of Minnesota doesn't look kindly upon repeat offenders, and I was in deep shit with all the charges and probation violations. I thought those five days in ADC were absolute hell, and now I was looking at months behind bars. My lawyer Chris told me the statute on a third DUI offense was a mandatory six months of jail.

Chris told me I needed to get myself into treatment immediately so when I did have my court appearance, at least it would appear to the judge that I was sober and getting my shit together. Coincidentally, I had at least a half dozen other friends facing DUI charges as well, so we decided to all go to the same treatment facility together.

When my court date finally arrived, my lawyer Chris came to the rescue like he always did and saved my ass. I received ninety days of house arrest and three years of probation—no jail time. I couldn't believe it! I'm not sure what Chris said during all those negotiations behind the closed chamber doors, but I didn't really care. If I didn't have to spend a night in jail, I was thankful and relieved.

The state also tried seizing my van since it was my third DUI offense, but because my mom's name was on the title, my attorneys managed to win that court hearing as well. It wasn't a total victory, though. The judge said I could keep the van, but I could never drive it again. Still, that was a better outcome than losing a $25,000 vehicle outright. I figured I'd just sell it, and once I was able to get my license reinstated, I would buy another vehicle.

Despite my good fortunes in court, my struggles continued. My ten-year high school reunion was coming up in a couple of weeks, and I was becoming extremely distressed about attending. I didn't want to skip it because all my friends were going, but I didn't want to relive my accident over again to the people from high school I hadn't seen since it happened. To make matters worse, I unintentionally agreed to turn myself in to get processed for house arrest the Monday following our reunion.

The reunion took place at the hotel and restaurant located right next door to my house, so I didn't have to worry about transportation getting there and back. It was a great time at first, but as the evening went on, it became increasingly depressing. There was a huge turnout of friends I hadn't seen since high school, but while everybody else got to talk about their accomplishments, I had to talk about how I ended up a quadriplegic.

As the night went on, I just got more despondent thinking about my senior year and how never in a million years could I have envisioned ten years ago that this was what my life would be like today. Talks with former classmates were incredibly uncomfortable.

When people asked what I did for a living, I'd think, "Oh, hey, Mitch—you're a lawyer now. Congratulations, I'm collecting disability," or, "Hello, Tina. You're married with two beautiful children. Awesome, I can barely achieve an erection." I didn't use those exact words, obviously, but that was basically the gist of my conversations.

All these people I went to school with were becoming successful professionals or starting families, and I was nothing but an invalid and a drain on society. I had nothing to show for the last ten years but lost hope and dreams and a bunch of court cases. I put on a fake smile and pretended everything was fine, but deep down, I was more dejected than ever over my accident.

As the night progressed, I started pounding the alcoholic beverages to numb myself to the explanations regarding my disability. Occasionally, I would go outside in the alley that led to my house and smoke some weed. Eventually, a friend went and picked up some cocaine, and the two of us started going back and forth from the reunion to my house to do lines of blow. The rest of my high school reunion was just a hazy cloud, and when it was over, my friend and I returned to my house to do more drugs.

The reunion was the proverbial straw that broke the camel's back—one big reminder of how the rug had been pulled out from under my life. After high school, the world had been mine, and I had everything a person could ask for. I was dating beautiful women, had dreams of playing golf professionally, and was athletic and outgoing, but what I got stuck with was permanent paralysis and a life in a wheelchair. To say I was feeling sorry for myself would be an understatement.

To bury the pain, I drank more liquor and did more cocaine all through the night and into the next day. Before I knew it, Saturday had turned into Monday morning, and in a couple of hours, I had to turn myself into the workhouse to be processed for house arrest.

My mind was racing, the cocaine crash was coming on hard, and my breath still smelled of rum and cokes. I didn't care, though. The reunion was such a harsh reminder of everything I lost, I just kept drinking and drugging. The prospect of jail time was nothing compared to the reality of spending the rest of my life in a wheel-chair. Still, I wasn't going to just give up. I had already beaten the system on several occasions, so I knew I could do it again.

When my sister arrived that morning to drive me to the workhouse, I told her to stop at GNC so I could buy some detoxifier. I wasn't sure it would even work with all the drugs coursing through my veins, but it was my only option. I drank the bottle of detoxifier along with a couple of bottles of water on my way to the workhouse, and then I just crossed my fingers and hoped for the best.

I arrived at the workhouse, and a guard sarcastically said, "Mr. Anderson, welcome back. Good to see you."

"Sorry, the feeling is not mutual," I replied.

"Well, quit fucking up! What the hell is your problem?"

"Ha, where should I start?"

The guard gave me a cup to urinate into and then proceeded to insert the paper drug testing strip. I watched anxiously, half expect-ing the strip to burst into flames from all the substances residing in my system. After several minutes, though, the guard said I passed. I was completely flabbergasted. Two hours earlier, I was snorting cocaine and smoking weed, yet somehow, I had just managed to pass another drug test.

For somebody who felt like the unluckiest person on earth, I sure was catching a lot of lucky breaks. I didn't look at it that way, though. I felt that my disability and shitty circumstances gave me the right to fuck off, and I blamed the state for putting me in situations that forced me to lie. I had a very unhealthy mindset at this stage after my accident, and all the drugs and alcohol were only impeding any rational or logical thinking.

My life was a double-edged sword. It didn't matter if I was sober or high on drugs; I still felt sad. That was especially true during my three months on house arrest. I had a lot of time on my hands to think about life and my recent decision-making. I also learned during this period that sobriety was not the answer to my problems. I was sober for twelve weeks and felt more depressed then I had at any other time in my life. Damned if I do, damned if I don't, I thought.

After my three months of house arrest ended, I sold my van and purchased a new vehicle in anticipation of getting my license reinstated. I was tired of driving minivans, so I sought out an alternative handicap vehicle. During my search on the internet, I discovered a Dodge pickup truck with a wheelchair conversion. It was candy apple red and had a wheelchair lift underneath the truck. It looked awesome and was exactly what I needed at the time to cure my ailing mental state.

The acquisition of my truck and the eventual reinstatement of my license changed things for me. I was so excited about driving again that I decided to sober up. I still used a little cocaine on occasion, but I pretty much quit drinking. To me, that was sober. I didn't want to do anything to risk losing my driver's license again, and alcohol was the main culprit behind all my driving infractions, so I didn't want to take any more risks by drinking.

In the summer of 2005, things were going well in my life for the first time since my accident eight years earlier. I applied for and accepted a part-time position working for a small credit union located in a nearby suburb. The credit union operated much differently than the large banks and corporations I had been employed with previously. Therefore, the work environment was more easy-going, and subsequently, my job was fun and less strenuous.

During the spring of 2006, a lot of my friends began to settle down and get married. I attended several bachelor parties and weddings, and I took several trips out of state for the various festivities. I kept my drinking to a minimum because I loved driving my new truck and was really enjoying my new job with the credit union. My friends weren't the only ones finding love, either. I returned to the dating scene at that time as well.

One night, I met a cute girl named Carrie at the bar. She was really cool, and we had a similar sense of humor. The next thing I knew, we were spending a lot of time together. We were always making out, and she even started spending the night a few days a week.

Despite all the fun we had together, though, there was a dark cloud continuously lurking over our relationship. Carrie was about seven years younger than me, pretty aggressive sexually, and I began to have a bad feeling that being intimate with her would inevitably lead to our undoing. To make matters worse, I was embarrassed to bring up the conversation about sex with her, and I got the sense that Carrie didn't want to ask about it either.

It wasn't like I didn't want to have sex. I was extremely attracted to Carrie, but to be honest, I was physically incapable of having sex at that time in my life. Over the last few years, the combination of prescription meds, drinking, drug use, and depression pretty much destroyed my libido and rendered me impotent. I couldn't tell Carrie any of this. It was highly emasculating, and I thought I would lose her entirely.

Instead, I carried on as if everything was fine and slowly watched as she and I drifted apart. It was all pretty tragic, especially since it was happening right when things in my life were starting to get good again. I had a new vehicle, a new job, a new girl, and a renewed spirit and semblance of normalcy, but all of that was beginning to unravel right before my eyes.

With the unraveling came the ghosts from my past—fear, anxiety, and despair. My newfound confidence was shattered, along with all the positivity that came with it. I only knew one way to cope with my problems, so I turned to drugs and alcohol again. I didn't know any other way to fight the demons of my disability.

As I began to spiral downwards, I met another girl who lifted me right back up. Her name was Lisa, and I met her at a small party at a friend's house. I remember thinking how beautiful she was, imagining that she would never be interested in somebody like me. After my failed relationship with Carrie, my confidence wasn't exactly at an all-time high.

However, a couple days after the party, I got a phone call from a friend who told me Lisa thought I was cute. I got Lisa's phone number and gave her a call one night, and the two of us talked for hours. I was still funny and charming, attributes my paralysis couldn't take from me, and shortly after our long phone conversation, Lisa and I went on our first date.

Ironically, while I was dating Lisa, I also started reconnecting with Carrie. Obviously, dating the two of them at once wasn't very monogamous or respectful, but I was relishing the newfound attention. I yearned for love and companionship, especially after witnessing so many of my friends getting married, so I didn't care. It wasn't like I was having sex with the two of them at the same time, so I didn't see any harm in it.

Inevitably, though, my inability to have sex doomed my relationship with both girls. I sought out the advice of a professional psychologist to salvage at least one of the relationships, but the psychologist confirmed what my doctor had already told me. My meds and issues with depression among other things were causing my impotence. Fixing the issue, I was told, would require changing up my prescriptions, undergoing months of counseling, sobriety, and a complete lifestyle change. It all seemed like such an obstacle to overcome.

Besides, I had no interest in quitting drugs and alcohol. I decided I'd rather quit dating. Drinking and partying were the only things I had going for me after my accident. Giving up fun would leave me with nothing, I felt. I wanted my cake and to eat it, too. I wanted to party and also be in a relationship with a girl. After everything I'd endured, I didn't think that was too much to ask for.

I eventually started drinking more and acting like an asshole because I knew both relationships were destined for failure. I chose self-sabotage over a meaningful relationship with either one of those beautiful girls. It was easier to just blow things up rather than try to fix my life. Essentially, I was choosing alcohol, drugs, and partying over a girlfriend because I still thought fun and friends were my only reprieve from my paralysis.

Even though it was my own doing, losing both Carrie and Lisa left me devastated. I watched all summer as my good friends got married and planned their futures and families. I was convinced that I would never find that special someone and experience true love again, and it was a harsh reminder of the loss of the perfect life I had before my accident.

Dealing with paralysis and my various other medical issues was hard enough. Dealing with the notion of never having a wife, kids, or family of my own was a whole other level of mental anguish. That summer, I took several steps forward, but I ultimately took even more steps backward. No matter what I did, I just couldn't live a normal life, so I decided I may as well burn it all down instead.

CHAPTER TWENTY-ONE

◆ ◆ ◆ ◆ ◆ ◆ ◆ ◆ ◆

Overdosed

WITH A BROKEN NECK AND now a broken heart, all the positive steps I made in the previous year were washed away in a sea of tears. I resumed my downward spiral and began ramping up my drug use. Ironically enough, I still appreciated my driving privileges and new truck enough to keep my alcohol consumption to a minimum.

I had restrictions on my driver's license that barred me from drinking alcohol, so I was highly conscious of where and when I decided to get drunk. Since the White Bear police knew who I was, I almost never got drunk or had more than a couple drinks if I was at a bar in my town. I was even nervous to drink at my own house since we still had people over there almost every weekend.

The problem was all my friends hung out in White Bear Lake pretty much all the time, and I was a targeted person at that point. I didn't want to risk getting caught drinking, so I decided to use cocaine whenever we went out instead. I was very sociable while on the drug, and it was a lot better than being sober.

My behavior was made easier by the fact that our dealer started hanging out with us. None of us really minded. He was a cool dude, and we were going to call him later those nights regardless. This made the drug more accessible. It was easier to have him party with us than to drive somewhere shady to meet him in the middle of the night.

However, with the cocaine came the nightmarish drug crashes, and I had never handled those well. The Valium I was taking completely mitigated the crash, but now that I was using it more frequently, I was burning through a thirty-day prescription of Valium in only a few days.

Without the Valium, I had to deal with my reality, and my reality was still filled with pain and misery. The cocaine would pick me up and let me forget my problems briefly, and the ensuing crash would always make me question my actions. The crash was only temporary, however, and my paralysis was permanent, so I kept on using more. It was this faulty reasoning that fueled my endless cycle of self-destruction.

One evening, we had people over at the house for a late-night gathering after bar close. Rick, our dealer, had called us earlier that day and told us he had some high-quality cocaine, and we were anxious to try it out. He met us all back at my house, and we started the festivities. We partied until the early morning, at which point almost everybody had left except for Rick and my good friend Jim.

We were all in my bedroom with the music still playing, arguing over a stupid internet scam of Rick's, when I wheeled over to my desk and snorted a line of coke the size of my finger. After partying all night, my tolerance would steadily increase, and subsequently, so would the amount and size of the lines I'd consume. There was nothing out of the ordinary about what I was doing compared to previous occasions.

The next thing I knew, though, I was opening my eyes and noticing an immensely bright light engulfing my bedroom. My vision was blurred, but as everything started to come back into focus, I saw the faces of my two friends standing above me, looking down on me with dreadful concern.

"Anderson. Anderson, can you hear me?" Jim asked frantically.

"Yeah, I can hear you—stop yelling!" I replied. "What the fuck am I doing on the floor?"

"You don't know what just happened?" Jim asked.

"No. Will you guys pick me up please, though?" I asked.

As my two friends lifted me off the floor and put me back into my wheelchair, I was still confused and disoriented, and it felt strangely like time had just stood still. After I regained a sense of normal consciousness, I asked them how I ended up falling out of my wheelchair. I had no recollection of time or anything—it felt like hours of the night had just gone missing.

They were both visibly shaken, and Jim started explaining how I had suddenly flopped out of my chair onto the ground and started going into seizure-like convulsions. He said my eyes rolled back into my head, and I lay there completely unconscious for a good few minutes. Then, still trembling from what had occurred, he got right up in my face.

In the most serious tone, he said emphatically, "I thought you were fucking dead, man!"

I could tell he was serious, but I still didn't believe what he was telling me—first, because I couldn't remember anything, and second, because what Jim was saying seemed so surreal, and I specifically didn't remember having any seizures. I looked at Rick, who was standing there all too calmly. When I asked him what had happened, he confirmed everything Jim was telling me.

I sat there in my chair, confused, and asked them both what they were doing while I was convulsing on the floor. Jim explained to me how he had quickly gathered up all the cocaine and rolled-up dollar bills so he could call 9-1-1, but Rick stopped him and told him he'd seen this same thing occur in one of the foster homes he grew up in.

"Don't call 9-1-1. He should come out of this," Rick had informed Jim as I lay on the floor convulsing, like he was an expert on the matter.

"What does that mean, you've seen this in foster homes?" Jim demanded.

"I was in foster homes with a lot of addicts," Rick explained to Jim. "This shit happened all the time. He should wake up in a few minutes."

I didn't know whether to be shocked or relieved to hear their version of events, so I just tried to take everything in stride. Regardless, I was back in my wheelchair and felt fine, so I told the guys to grab the coke and set out some more lines.

"You can't be fucking serious!" Jim said, disconcerted.

"Yeah, I'm dead serious," I replied. "Why not?"

"You just nearly died, dude!" Jim yelled in my face.

I wasn't exactly sure what had happened to me as I went into seizures on my bedroom floor, but to be honest, I didn't even care. I was starting to come down fast, and I wanted to do another line then more than anything. The only thing I cared about was doing more drugs, and nothing else mattered—this is what my life had come to.

I was oblivious to the drug overdose that I had experienced a few minutes before, just as I was ignorant of the self-destruction I had been inflicting on my body over the last few months. The only thing I could think about was the bag of cocaine still in my house and the impending drug crash that I desperately wanted to avoid.

That was the disturbing power of the drug in its most unadulterated form—the ability to bring me so high that once I started my journey back down, I would do almost anything for more drugs just to avoid the depression that would shortly follow. I wanted to avoid the daunting reality that constantly haunted my life, along with the crash that I would experience if I didn't keep my high going.

I demanded that Rick bring me the bag of cocaine, but Jim was insistent that I not do any more drugs. He even threatened to leave.

"Fine. Get the fuck out of here," I demanded. "More drugs for us!"

"You're out of your mind, Anderson," Jim responded angrily.

Rick retrieved the bag of blow that Jim had hidden in my closet and proceeded to chop up a couple more lines on my desk. I grabbed the rolled-up dollar bill, snorted a line, and then began to shake uncontrollably, falling to the floor once again. Jim and Rick were in a state of panic and got on their knees, shaking me repeatedly.

"Oh, my God. Oh, my God! Anderson, Anderson, are you OK?" Jim asked frantically.

That's when I opened my eyes and started laughing hysterically. "Got you, motherfuckers!" I exclaimed with a shit-eating grin on my face.

"Are you out of your mind, Anderson?" Jim yelled angrily. "Not cool at all! You're fucking crazy. I'm out of here." He ran out the back door, slamming it behind him.

"Come on, Jim—don't be like that," I yelled back. "It was just a joke." However, he was already gone.

Rick picked me up and put me back in my wheelchair while the two of us chuckled at my sick and depraved prank.

"That was pretty fucked up, dude." Rick said to me half-heartedly.

"I know," I replied. "It was kind of funny, though—you have to admit."

"Yeah, it was pretty funny. I'll give you that." The two of us laughed again.

With Jim gone, Rick and I continued to party. He and I were two peas in a pod when it came to cocaine, so I knew he had no problem continuing our night of debauchery. The two of us would finish off every last particle of drugs even if a tornado ripped my house from its foundation. There was just no stopping us. The words "consequences" and "ramifications" were foreign to us in that frame of mind.

Rick and I kept partying until early afternoon, and when the cocaine was gone, I felt the devil's grip tightening around me fast. Rick took off on his Vespa, and I was left alone with nothing but my thoughts and regrets. Whatever sense of humor I had while doing drugs was soon replaced with thoughts of despair as the drug crash began to take hold.

There was no way I could deal with the anxiety, depression, and anguish after everything that had occurred over the past twenty-four hours. Whenever I had to battle through these crashes after a coke binder, all I did was think about negative shit, and I just couldn't handle those emotions hours after experiencing a drug overdose. I needed to get more drugs so I didn't have to face reality or feel emotion. I had to put off that crash any way I could!

I called up another good friend of mine, a veteran I knew had prescriptions for multiple types of benzodiazepines to help treat his PTSD. With desperation in my voice, I explained my situation to him, and he gladly came over and dropped off about a half dozen high milligram Xanax. After he left, I took them all at once, washing them down with a can of warm beer still sitting on my counter.

After contemplating how many pills I had just taken, I started to second-guess myself, worried that maybe I had taken a tad too many. Before the pills had even a second to kick in, I started to get extremely anxious and paranoid. I begin to wheel around in intense circles, which was my version of pacing back and forth, as I thought about my next move. I started to worry about experiencing a second overdose, one that I might not wake up from.

I decided to call Carrie instead of 9-1-1 and ask her for help. She and I had done drugs together on a few occasions in the past, so I knew she'd understand. Besides, the two of us had recently started hanging out again, and she was becoming a great friend I could trust. Given that I was on probation, I didn't want the police at my house, so I figured she was the next best option.

Thankfully, Carrie answered her phone and agreed to come over and help me in my frenzied condition. By the time she arrived, though, all those Xanax had kicked in, and I was in a heavy state of sedation. My fear and despair gradually turned to eerie calmness. I explained about my overdose early that morning as well as all the Xanax I took. I told Carrie I just wanted to go to sleep but was concerned I might not wake up, so I asked her to check on me every few minutes.

This was further proof of how twisted my mind was at that time. If I was so concerned about overdosing on pills, I should have called 9-1-1, not another drug user. My thought process was irrational, though, and always resulted in a convoluted mess of incoherent behavior that unavoidably resulted in more drug use. I didn't want to deal with my disability, so I did drugs. To escape the crash that using cocaine inevitably brought on, I simply did more drugs.

Carrie helped me into bed, and as soon as my back hit the mattress, I was fast asleep. When I awoke a few hours later, all I could hear was loud music, laughter, and the voices of screaming girls coming from my living room. I transferred into my chair, wheeled into the hallway, and went around the corner only to discover pandemonium.

There were empty bottles of Jägermeister and cans of Red Bull strewn around the kitchen, and two girls dressed only in their underwear were dancing on my furniture. Carrie came running over to me, jumped on my lap, and started talking to me in some form of gibberish, too fast for me to understand. Eventually, I was able to pick up that Rick was arrested for driving a stolen Vespa and needed bail money, and Carrie had invited her friend over to keep her company while she watched over me.

Carrie then informed me they had gotten drunk on Jägermeister and decided to get some cocaine as well. Considering the circumstances, all I could do was laugh. I was just thankful to be alive, especially knowing that Carrie probably forgot she was at my house to check on my well-being, not to party. My brain was fried at that point. Trying to fathom everything that was happening around me was literally giving me a headache. I felt like Alice going down the rabbit hole.

I went back into my bedroom, lay down in bed, and proceeded to think about the events that had unfolded over the last forty-eight hours. I cursed myself and then cursed God for giving me this life. I cried tears of guilt and shame, knowing my actions would crush my mom if she ever found out what I was doing to myself. I silently stared at the ceiling, telling myself over and over that this was the last time I would use cocaine. Unfortunately, that was a lie I was becoming all too comfortable with.

CHAPTER TWENTY-TWO

◆ ◆ ◆ ◆ ◆ ◆ ◆ ◆ ◆

More Bad Luck

THE OVERDOSE INCIDENT THAT WEEKEND really shook me up. Most stories I had heard of people overdosing usually ended badly. I kept dwelling on the fact that if I did indeed overdose that morning, then I just as easily could have died. I still wasn't completely sure that's what had happened, though—I certainly wasn't going to take the word of my drug dealer as a diagnosis.

I decided to ask a good friend of mine who was an ER nurse to find out for sure. Given his experience working in an emergency room, he should know what happened to me. I saw my nurse friend at a party one night and took him aside, explaining everything that had taken place that weekend.

After describing how I had fallen onto my bedroom floor and gone into convulsions, I asked him sincerely, "Do you know what happened to me?"

"Jesus, Anderson!" he exclaimed. "Yeah, I know what happened. You overdosed! You're really lucky."

"Are you positive that's what happened?" I reiterated.

"Yes, I'm sure. I'm an ER nurse. I see a lot of overdoses!"

"Damn. Well, is there anything I should do?" I asked, concerned.

"Yeah. You should quit fucking doing drugs!" he said bluntly.

He made a good point, there was no denying that, and I did quit doing drugs for a good few weeks after that. I quit doing a lot of things, for that matter. I became withdrawn and morose for a period of time. I couldn't stop thinking about almost dying—it seemed so surreal. Now all I kept thinking about was my screwed-up life and the fucked-up games God continued to play with me. Why was I still here? Was there some grand plan for me that was still unfulfilled?

After a while, though, my mind began to settle down, and I gradually started going out again. I was still scared of losing my license, so I was careful whenever I drank alcohol. Also, I had a new doctor now, and she was hesitant to prescribe me Valium, so I was trying to minimize my use of cocaine. I was afraid of the horrendous crashes that always ensued.

I still had people over a lot on the weekends because of my proximity to the bars, so there was partying going on at my house rather consistently. One evening I had a bunch of people over after the bar closed as usual. I wasn't drinking because I was driving the truck around most of the night. I did do a couple lines of cocaine at the house, but I went to bed earlier than usual while everybody else stayed up and partied.

I woke up a few hours later as the sun began to rise because I heard people in the living room, and I discovered that my friend and his girlfriend were still there. The two of them were bickering over which one of them was in better shape to drive. Even though I was still rather tired, I told them I would drive the two of them home since I was the only sober one there.

We stopped at my friend's house first so he could grab some things, and then we headed toward his girlfriend's place, where I was going to drop them off. It was a beautiful late summer morning, and the street was bustling with kids walking to school and parents on their way to work. My windows were down, and I remember feeling calm and at peace, probably because I was getting my two drunk friends home safely and doing something right for once.

As I drove down the busy road, I noticed the driver in front of me put on their right turn signal and begin to slow down. I patiently waited for the car to turn, but as I got closer, I noticed the driver was stopped in the middle of the road, not turning as their signal indicated they were going to do. Fearing a rear-end collision, I made a split-second decision to go around the car to avoid hitting it.

I didn't want to pass on their right side because I was afraid the car might still turn and crash into me, so I decided to go around the left and I turned into the center lane. Out of the corner of my eye, I saw two kids run from the sidewalk into the middle of the street. I tried to swerve and miss the children, but when they saw me, the two of them ran back in the same direction. I swerved again, but the kids reacted the same way as well.

That's when I felt a crash and heard the most disturbing sound my ears had ever experienced. Time stood still in that instant. Everything was frozen, everything went silent, and my mind went completely blank. I couldn't believe it—I had just struck two little kids in the middle of the street with my big truck.

I was so scared that, for a brief second, I thought about stepping on the gas and fleeing. Almost instantly, I realized how foolish that would be. Instead, I pulled over to the side of the road, but when I looked into my rearview mirror, I saw the kids lying motionless in the street. Immediately, I thought they were dead, and the most eerie feeling I had ever felt rushed over my body. I had just killed two little kids. How could this be happening?

"Oh, my God. Oh, my God. Let me out of here!" my friend's girl-friend said as she burst open my truck door and started running through somebody's backyard.

My buddy stepped out of the truck and yelled after her. "Get back here now! Where the fuck do you think you're going?"

"Oh, my God. What did I do?" I asked fearfully. "This can't be happening."

"Everybody calm the fuck down!" said my friend. "Anderson, those kids came running out of nowhere. It's not your fault." He did his best to reassure me. "Everything is going to be OK."

After taking a few deep breaths, I picked up my phone and dialed 9-1-1, but I was told by the operator they'd already received several calls about the accident. While I was on the phone, my friend was consoling his girlfriend out on the sidewalk, after convincing her to return to my truck. I knew those two had been up all-night partying, so I just told them both to get out of there. I figured the last thing they wanted to see was the police, whose sirens I could already hear coming in the distance.

Only two or three minutes had passed since I struck the two children, but for me, it seemed like an eternity. I waited anxiously for the ambulance to arrive, watching in my rearview mirror as good Samaritans tended to the two kids lying in the road. My truck was so big, and those children seemed so small. I kept replaying that crashing sound in my mind. It was the worst sound I had ever heard, and the most distressing thoughts were racing through my mind.

Finally, an ambulance arrived, along with several police cars. Some of the officers approached the scene of the accident, and several others pulled up directly behind me. I rolled down my window as a few troopers approached my truck and asked me for my driver's license and proof of insurance. When I handed the closest officer my information, his partner breathed a sigh of relief.

"Thank God you have insurance," he said.

Another officer approached my window and asked me what happened, so I explained how the car in front of me had just stopped in the middle of the street and how I tried to go around it. By this point, it was very chaotic at the accident scene, with several cars parked along the sides of the road and dozens of people gathering in the streets. My heart was racing, and I just kept asking the officers if the children were OK.

One of the officers walked back up to my window with a breath-alyzer in hand, which didn't surprise me at all. I knew the police were going to test me for alcohol, especially with my prior DUIs. I blew into the tube as hard as I could and passed the test, which I fully expected. I asked the officer again if the kids were going to be OK, but they still wouldn't give me an answer.

I couldn't just sit there doing nothing, so I called my mother and frantically told her I was just in an accident and had hit some kids. She kept telling me to calm down, that accidents happen all the time. I could tell she thought I hit another vehicle.

I finally just said to her, "Mom, you don't understand. I hit the kids while they were crossing the street."

At that moment, there was a scary silence that lasted for several seconds. My mom was so aghast at what I just told her that for once in her life, she was at a complete lost for words.

"Well, are they OK?" she asked anxiously.

"I don't know," I answered, now sobbing uncontrollably. "I think I might have killed them."

"Oh, my God. You weren't drinking, were you?" she asked.

"No!" I exclaimed. "I was driving drunk friends."

"Where are you? I'm on my way now."

I told my mother where I was and continued to watch the chaos unfold in my rearview mirror. The only thing I cared about was the kids, but since the police weren't telling me anything, I started to think about my situation in more depth.

I had passed a breathalyzer no problem, but if the cops decided to take a blood sample, I was fucked. I may have been sober when I was driving, but there were drugs in my system from the night before, and that's all that would matter in the eyes of the court. The severity and enormity of the accident started weighing on me heavily. I was already scared for the children, but now I was becoming concerned with what might become of me, so I called my lawyer Chris and explained what had occurred.

The first thing Chris asked me was the same thing my mother did—if I had been drinking. I answered with a resounding no, so Chris told me not to worry then—it was just an accident. I told him I had smoked some weed the night before, not wanting to be completely honest with him about the drugs. That's when he snapped.

"Goddammit, Eric!" he said angrily. "When are you going to fucking learn your lesson?"

Chris was pissed that I kept putting myself in those situations. He was thankful I wasn't drinking, but he was adamant that I shouldn't be doing any drugs, period. If I wanted to legally drive in the state, then I had to abstain from drugs and alcohol, and not just some of the time—all of the time. He reminded me that that was the deal I had made with the state.

Chris had to be in court, but he told me that he was going to get in touch with John and apprise him of the situation. If the police told me they needed a blood sample or anything else, I should call John immediately. He could tell I was in a state of sheer terror and did his best to assure me everything was going to be fine. That was easy for him to say—he wasn't the one who had just hit two kids with a truck.

As I hung up my phone, I saw the ambulance speed away with the children inside as several officers approached my truck. One of them handed me my license and insurance, and again, I asked them if the children were going to be OK. That's when an officer told me both kids were going to live, but one of them was injured pretty badly.

Right about that time, my mom pulled up to the accident scene and came rushing over to me. I was still shaken and burst into tears as soon as I saw her. I told her this was the worst thing I had ever experienced—even worse than my accident. I had struck trees in the past, along with fences, garbage cans, and other cars, but there is nothing like the sound of crashing into human beings. I told her I would never forget that sound, and if either of those children were permanently injured, I wasn't sure I could live with that.

The police informed me there was nothing else they needed from me and that I could go. They did say somebody may contact me down the road, but I was just relieved they weren't wanting a blood sample. I assumed they were convinced that the incident was nothing but a tragic accident, which it was. After that, all I could think about was the what-ifs. What if we had left my house five minutes later, what if I had driven a different route, or worse yet, what if the kids die or end up paralyzed?

Once I was home, I broke down and cried while my mom hugged me and tried to tell me everything was going to be OK. I could just picture the mothers of the children doing the same for them in the hospital at that very moment. My mom then advised me to notify my insurance company. Given the circumstances, it seemed like the right thing to do. I didn't really want to relive the events that had just unfolded, but I figured I should get it over with.

I got in touch with my insurance agent and told him about the accident. As I was describing what had happened, he informed me that he had already read about it on the news. I couldn't believe it. I wasn't too surprised it made the news, but I was just surprised it made the news so quickly. It had only been a couple of hours since the accident. How could the media possibly have all the facts?

Later in the day, I reluctantly turned on the afternoon news and saw coverage of the accident. Every channel was leading with the story about two children on their way to school getting mowed down by some maniacal young driver. In their descriptions, I drove recklessly through the streets of White Bear Lake, leaving a trail of carnage and destruction in my wake. That was literally the context of their reporting, and much of what they were reporting was inaccurate.

I called my lawyer John and told him about the misleading news coverage. I asked him if I could call the media and give them my side of the story, but he answered with a resounding no. John explained that anything I said to the media could be used against me in court down the road if I got charged with any violations. He told me to keep my mouth shut, turn off the news, and try to get some rest. There was nothing I could do now.

Emotionally, I was a train wreck. I kept playing the accident over again in my head, along with the sound of crashing into those two children. It was driving me insane not knowing if they were going to be OK or not. I called a few friends and tried watching a movie—anything to keep my mind occupied by something other than the accident. Nothing worked, though. I was too worried about those kids, and I had to get more information.

I decided to call a good friend of mine who used to be a nurse but now worked at the hospital in administration. I explained the situation to her and told her that I was concerned for the children's well-being and desperate for information. My friend could tell I was rather upset about the whole ordeal. Even though it was probably against hospital rules, she sympathized with me and the kids and told me she would see what she could find out about their conditions.

My friend called me back later that night to give me an update on the children's status. She informed me one of the kids had been released from the hospital with a broken arm, but the other one was in more serious condition. He had several broken bones and some internal injuries, but she told me with some certainty that he should make a full recovery after extensive rehab.

I was somewhat relieved because it sounded as if they hadn't sustained any permanent injuries, but I didn't like not knowing the exact prognosis of the more severely injured child. Regardless, as much as it bothered me to not know exactly what their future held, all I could do at that point was hope and pray for the best.

CHAPTER TWENTY-THREE

◆ ◆ ◆ ◆ ◆ ◆ ◆ ◆ ◆

Bedrock

THE SUN IS SHINING BRIGHT on a warm sunny day. I'm driving a red convertible along the lake, and there's a beautiful blonde sitting in the passenger seat. She's wearing big sunglasses and red lipstick, and her hair is blowing in the wind. She looks just like Courtney. The music is playing loud, I have a huge smile on my face, and everything is perfect. That's when I see two kids come running into the street. I crash into them both, sending them flying into the air. Then I awaken with my heart pounding through my chest.

This was the dream that haunted my sleep night after night since that accident. When I wasn't sleeping, I was reliving the incident with those children in my head all throughout the day. I stopped praying. I even stopped believing God existed. What kind of God would let all this bad shit happen to a person? Furthermore, my own problems paled in comparison to the death, destruction, and misery that permeated the globe. I was pissed off at the world.

I started drinking a lot. Although I wasn't drinking and driving, I no longer cared about the alcohol restrictions on my driver's license. With the drinking and partying came more drug use, and the cocaine sent my anxiety levels through the roof. In turn, my insomnia was exasperated by all the drugs. I was stressed, irritable, and in need of Valium. I needed more Valium badly!

I had given up on trying to get my new doctor to refill my prescription. She was very reluctant in the past and told me she had serious concerns about prescribing me benzos. I suspect she knew I had issues with substance abuse. I may have been good at hiding things from friends and family members, but I assume the warning signs were more than obvious to her.

However, after I told her about the accident with the children and how I was having major problems with anxiety and insomnia, she was shocked. That incident seemed to convince her of a true medical need. She refilled my prescription for Valium, referred me to a psychologist, and then transferred me to a different doctor. She no longer wanted to treat me, and I couldn't blame her.

When I picked up my prescription from the pharmacy after my appointment, I noticed the bottle was heavier than usual. I took it out of the bag and saw it was filled to the top. At first, I thought the pharmacy had made an error. When I glanced at the label, it read 120 Valium and eight refills. I couldn't believe my eyes.

I had never been good at math, but at that moment, I instantly turned into Albert Einstein. I quickly did the math in my head and knew that was nearly a thousand Valium pills. I felt like I was reading the winning numbers to a Powerball lottery ticket. I could now completely numb all my pain and do all the coke I wanted without any ramifications from the dreadful crash that always ensued. If my life had a self-destruct button, I was just about to push it.

I went on a rampage after that, going to the bars every night and having people over afterwards. I was doing coke, popping pills, and then sleeping all day. I started calling into work frequently or going in late, still using my disability as an excuse as I had in the past. Even if I had gotten fired, I wouldn't have cared. I didn't care about anything at that time. Not only was my body paralyzed, my feelings were as well. I was becoming completely detached from life.

After one weekend of partying and coke, I went into work at the credit union on Monday morning and discovered that it was time for my annual review. I had completely forgotten it was coming. Whenever we had our reviews, our managers would take us to a nice restaurant for lunch and discuss our progress and shortcomings, setting new goals going forward. Normally I would be excited, but on this particular day, I was completely caught off guard. The last thing I wanted to do was sit in front of my two bosses discussing my work history after being up for two days on a coke binge.

I tried to play it cool, but as I sat there discussing my job performance with my two managers, blood started pouring from my nose. I couldn't believe it. My manager quickly wetted a napkin and handed it to me, and I wheeled into the bathroom as quickly as possible to get the bleeding under control. After several minutes, I finally got the bleeding to stop and wheeled back to the table

"Stupid allergies," I said, embarrassed.

Allergies in the dead of winter were hardly believable, but what else was I supposed to say? I could only hope that they were naïve enough not to think my nose bleed was anything drug related. That moment was a harsh reminder of just how much I was letting my drug use get the best of me. Still, I had no intention of dialing things back. Got to pay to play, I thought.

Things only got worse later that week when I received several tickets related to the accident with the children. It turns out there was a crosswalk in the street, which is why the car was stopped in front of me. However, I never saw the crosswalk. Furthermore, I had driven down that road a thousand times before, and nobody had ever abruptly stopped to let people cross. I was only focused on the car stopped in front of me with its turn signal on, so I didn't notice the kids until it was too late.

I informed my attorney John of the tickets, and he prepared me for my eventual court hearing. John advised me to make my probation officer aware of the accident, which I did shortly thereafter. When I told Grumpy about it, he was actually shocked and somewhat saddened. He told me he didn't feel the accident constituted a probation violation, and I was relieved and surprised. Grumpy had a heart after all.

When my court day arrived, my mother accompanied me to the courthouse. My attorney Chris worked out a plea bargain that was acceptable to all the parties involved. After pleading guilty to careless driving, I asked the judge if I could say something to the family of the children who were sitting behind me. The judge agreed to let me make a statement but told me to address the court instead of the families directly.

With my lips quivering, my voice cracking, and tears pouring from my eyes, I explained to the judge how deeply sorry I was. I explained how the car abruptly stopped in front of me, that I never saw the crosswalk, and how everything happened so fast. I told the court about the persistent nightmares and that I thought of the children every day. I begged and pleaded for their forgiveness as I sobbed uncontrollably.

There was hardly a dry eye in the courtroom that morning. The judge stated how overwhelmed he was by the amount of empathy, respect, and decency all parties were demonstrating to one another. Even though the judge had instructed me not to address the parents, I whispered how sorry I was to them all as I wheeled by them on my way out of court. I needed to look them in the eyes when I said it so they would know I was sincere.

After my court appearance, I tried to sober up as best as I could. I went to the bars occasionally, but I wasn't using any cocaine. I concentrated on work, completed my community service, and stayed away from any situation that could compromise my attempt at sobriety. I even started speaking at schools again. I was sincerely trying to make a concerted effort to turn my life around. I felt I owed it to those kids and their families.

One evening, I agreed to meet my mother and godmother down-town for dinner to celebrate their birthdays. As I drove down the highway, a stoplight suddenly turned yellow as I approached the intersection. Since I was so close to the intersection and still had the right of way, I just continued because it was too late to stop.

As I did, I noticed a van approach from the opposite direction and abruptly take a left-hand turn right in front of me. I slammed on my brakes, but to no avail. My truck T-boned the van at a relatively high speed. The collision was violent and loud, and the dust from the exploding airbags filled the cab of my truck like smoke from a fire.

As I gathered my composure and the dust began to settle, I noticed my knees were pinned underneath my dash. My jeans were ripped, and there was blood all over my legs. A witness at the scene pried open the passenger door and forcefully entered my truck to help me. He attempted to free up my legs, but they were pinned underneath the hand controls attached to my dash and pedals. He kept asking me if I was OK, but I was in complete shock.

I just sat there feeling blank as emergency vehicles and bystanders gathered around me. There were sirens wailing and commotion everywhere, but I just sat there in silence. As the police arrived, a female officer walked up to the passenger side of my vehicle and switched places with the gentlemen who was still trying to help me.

"Hi, Eric," she said. "Do you remember me?"

"No," I answered, confused.

"I was at the accident you had with the children," she explained. "Have you ever considered quitting driving?"

Normally, I would have been offended by her question. I should have the right to drive the same as everybody else. After all my accidents, however, I was beginning to feel cursed and replied somberly, "Actually, I was just sitting here pondering that."

I was a broken man after that accident. My spirit was crushed to pieces, just like my truck. I couldn't understand how I could possibly be so unlucky. Granted, I brought on some of my own misfortune, but that van had turned left right in front of me—I had the right of way, for crying out loud. That shit wasn't my fault. I wasn't drunk or impaired. I just couldn't catch a break no matter what I did.

The relentless waves of emotions were taking their toll on me, not to mention all the different drugs and alcohol I was consuming. I couldn't imagine the chemical imbalances taking place in my brain. I tried like hell to keep it together, I really did, but it didn't take much to push me over the edge. Sometimes the most inconsequential things could trigger repressed memories and send me spiraling into a drunken bender.

One afternoon, I decided to spend the day on the lake on my friend's boat. It was a warm summer day, and the sun felt so good on my face and neck. We boated from beach to beach, meeting up with different people we knew. It was only the second or third time I'd been on the lake since my accident, so it was a nice reprieve from the stress and daily depression I constantly battled. I was really enjoying the day, right up to the point I noticed Carrie on another boat hanging all over some guy, kissing and being overly flirtatious.

I tried to act cool and pretend I wasn't bothered, but it was one of those moments that triggered very strong emotions—jealousy first, then rage, and then pure sadness. I wasn't upset that Carrie was with some other guy. I was upset because I didn't have a hot girl hanging all over me on my boat like I had the entire summer before my accident. Of all the places to see her—in the middle of a big fucking lake! I fumed at my constant bad luck.

I started downing drinks and continued until the early evening, doing shot after shot of tequila until I blacked out. When I did come to, my drunk friend was pushing me down the highway in a desperate attempt to get me home. My house was nearly three miles from the bar, so it was probably a bit foolhardy to try and make the journey by foot—especially in our condition. I never questioned our actions, though. I was too shit-faced.

As the two of us made our way along the side of the road, the asphalt became very rough and uneven. My legs were bouncing around, and my feet kept falling off my wheelchair. I was trying to hold my legs steady when my front wheels hit a deep crack in the street, stopping my chair abruptly. I went flying face-first into the pavement, split my head wide open, and was knocked unconscious.

The next thing I knew, I was coming to in the front seat of a truck with several squad cars surrounding the vehicle. My friend and his mom were arguing with the police, so I quickly concluded we were in his driveway. I was disoriented and had blood all over my shirt and shorts. The police kept asking me if I wanted an ambulance, but I just kept telling them I wanted to go home.

After the chaos in the yard settled down, the police focused their attention on me.

"Eric, do you need an ambulance?" an officer asked.

"No, I just want to go home," I replied, annoyed.

"Are you sure? That's a pretty nasty gash you have on your head."

"I'm fine. I just want to go home."

"OK, but we need you to blow in a breathalyzer first."

"Why? I wasn't driving."

"Because we don't feel you're in any type of condition to make a reasonable decision," the officer told me.

I kept refusing to blow into a breathalyzer, but the police kept insisting. Even in my inebriated state, I couldn't help but think they were trying to set me up for something. I refused their repeated requests over and over, but the officers maintained it was for my own well-being.

Eventually, their persistence wore me down, and I acquiesced to their demands. I blew into the breathalyzer and my blood alcohol content was nearly a point-three-zero. After that insanely high reading, the police were adamant I was not capable of making rational decisions for myself, so they called an ambulance to come transport me to the ER. Even I was a bit shocked by how high the breathalyzer reading was, so I didn't put up much of a fight.

The rest of the night was pretty much a blur. I had a slight concussion and needed ten stiches to close the cut on my forehead. My mother and step-dad met me down at the emergency room and were not happy with my behavior. I was acting loud and belligerent, cracking stupid jokes and thinking I was a comedian. Nobody in the ER found my antics amusing. It was not one of my proudest moments, and come morning, I felt like I had been run over by a semi-truck.

Two weeks later, I received a letter in the mail from the Department of Public Safety informing me my driver's license had been cancelled for three years. This was a result of getting caught drinking while I had alcohol restrictions on my license. I knew that's why the police wanted to breathalyze me so badly—they wanted to bust me. Still, I had nobody to blame but myself.

From that point on, things went from bad to worse. Even though I drank and partied when I had a valid driver's license, the alcohol restrictions kept me somewhat in check. I was always afraid of losing my driving privileges, so I was typically careful and exercised restraint when it came to drinking. None of that mattered anymore. Now that I couldn't drive for three years, I felt I had free reign to do whatever the hell I wanted.

Furthermore, my mom and step-dad left for Mexico for two months like they did every winter. With them out of the country and my driver's license cancelled, there was nothing holding me back. I could do all the drinking and drugs I desired while I wallowed in my own self-pity. At that point, I was highly proficient in feeling sorry for myself. There was no light at the end of the tunnel anymore. All I saw was darkness.

Over the next couple of months, I kept up my nefarious behavior and continued to self-implode my life. At one point, I ended up in the psych ward at the hospital on a seventy-two-hour hold because I consumed far too many Valium and my sister had to call 9-1-1. A couple of weeks after that, my roommate found me passed out on my deck in sub-zero temperatures, nearly frozen to death. As if that wasn't enough, a friend of mine left my house drunk and high on pills after a party one night and crashed his jeep into a telephone poll in my alleyway.

When my parents returned from Mexico, my sister told them about everything that had happened while they were gone. My mom and step-dad were livid—and rightly so. They were accustomed to the carnage I was inflicting on my life, but it was the accident my friend got into while leaving my house that really set them off. That type of incident results in lawsuits, and they had had enough.

One weekend morning, my mom came over to help me shower and get dressed because I wasn't feeling well. After getting my clothes on, I wheeled out of my room and saw a horde of people gathered together in the living room. I was shocked, not at the intervention that was about to take place, but at how they had all gotten into the house so quickly and silently, like a bunch of ninjas. This was a ninja intervention, I thought.

Family members, my godmother, and even my lawyer John all took turns telling me how concerned they were for my well-being. It was nice knowing so many people cared, but I was very combative. I reminded them all of the perfect life I had before my accident and everything I lost with my paralysis. I justified my drug use, even though I downplayed it considerably. In the end, though, my family gave me an ultimatum: get help or find a new place to live.

I sought out help, toned down the partying, and did pretty well for a few months after that. It was just enough to get my mom off my back. However, I ended up getting a new roommate, and he was the worst kind of enabler. He was also one of the funniest, most entertaining people I knew, so it was too difficult not to party with him. He actually brought some joy into my otherwise fucked-up life.

Unfortunately, he had drug issues of his own and was traveling down a similar path to rock bottom.

In the end, my friend went away to treatment after we both lost our jobs in the housing market crash of 2008. I loved my job at the credit union, so I was absolutely devastated when I was let go. I thought it was the only good thing I had left going well in my life, so I responded in the only manner I knew how and ramped up the partying and drug use once again to mask my despair.

I spent so much time sitting in my wheelchair doing cocaine—sometimes for two or three days straight—that eventually I ended up with a bedsore on my butt. When I was in the hospital after my accident, the nurses had constantly reminded me about pressure relief and avoiding bedsores at all cost. They can become infected and cause sepsis, and people can even die from them. I had ignored their warnings, however, and now I had to deal with another self-inflicted major health and life issue.

The only way to heal a pressure wound is to stay off it, so I had to lie on my stomach constantly for two months, twenty-two hours a day. I only got up to eat, shower, and go to the bathroom. Otherwise, I was alone, isolated, and confined to my room almost the entire summer. The boredom was mind-numbing, and my despair only deepened.

I didn't do any drugs or alcohol for eight weeks as I tried to heal my bedsore, yet ironically, I was more depressed than ever. I hated my life with every fiber of my being, and I had eight weeks to constantly dwell on my misfortune. If that wasn't rock bottom, it was as close as I could get. At the very least, I felt like I had hit bedrock. How could I possibly sink any lower?

CHAPTER TWENTY-FOUR

◆ ◆ ◆ ◆ ◆ ◆ ◆ ◆

EDM Saved Me

AS SOON AS MY PRESSURE sore healed, I picked up right where I left off with my partying and drug use. Being cooped up in bed for eight weeks only fueled my desire to let loose and have some fun to take my mind off my problems. However, my mechanism of escape was a recipe for disaster. I thought I needed the clubs, socializing, and drugs to cure what ailed me, but the partying was working against me in the most unfavorable ways.

Soon, I had no more Valium. I went through all my refills, and my doctor had no interest in prescribing any more. Without the Valium, I had to struggle with the awful drug crash and the anguish that always followed. You would think this would cause me to dial down the partying, but it didn't. Don't get me wrong—every night after doing a bunch of blow, I would swear to myself I was finished. Eventually, though, I'd catch up on my sleep, head out to the bar again, and end up back in my room snorting lines of cocaine off my desk.

The cycle really went into overdrive when I decided to start dealing drugs. It happened very unexpectedly. After having drinks one night with one of our coke suppliers, I told him I had lost my job at the credit union and was unemployed. He immediately told me he had a way for me to make some extra cash. He knew I had a bunch of friends who did cocaine, and he wanted to take advantage of my long list of potential consumers.

He offered to front me a half ounce of coke every week. He would stop by every Friday to pick up his cash and drop off another half ounce. As usual, I was completely oblivious to all the potential consequences and thought it sounded like a great idea. The unemployment I was collecting at the time didn't pay that much, so I thought it was a great way to supplement my income. Besides, I'd also have free cocaine for myself, saving me a considerable amount of money.

Furthermore, I had always had a fascination with the black market and underground economy. I was always watching gangster movies and listening to hip-hop music that constantly glorified drug dealing, so for me, that was part of the allure. However, everybody knows the golden rule for a drug dealer: never get high off your own supply. My new business endeavor was a complete disaster right from the start—I was doing way more cocaine than I was selling.

With such an abundant supply at my house, my drug use expanded from only on the weekends to almost every day. Somehow, I was still convinced that I could control my habit and turn a profit. I would have my good friend come over and help me weigh up and bag the drugs, and I would give him some free blow for helping me out. I'd take a little bit for myself and then instruct my friend to hide the rest in the garage so I wouldn't do it all.

After staying up for a day or two finishing the coke I had set aside for personal use, I would go down to my garage and rip it apart looking for the rest of it. Like a drug-sniffing dog, I always found it, too. It didn't matter where my friend hid the supply; I was like a fucking bloodhound when it came to finding my stash. I was relentless, doing anything to avoid the crash.

When hiding the drugs in the garage didn't work, I decided to change tactics and had my friend put all the cocaine in a basement closet. My thinking was that since I was in a wheelchair and couldn't get downstairs, I wouldn't be able to get to it. Never underestimate the creativity and ingenuity of a drug addict, though.

My drug crashes started to become so severe I would do almost anything to avoid them. I would literally throw myself out of my wheelchair and call a friend to come pick me off the floor. Once they arrived and got me back into my chair, I would have them go downstairs and retrieve the bag with all the cocaine. Once I started, I couldn't stop, and if the drugs were in my house, I was going to get to them one way or another

Prior to all that, my cocaine use was still pretty much recreational, albeit frequent. Now, however, I was officially out of control, and it was fueling a raging inferno of depression inside me. Every line of cocaine was like gasoline thrown on a fire of misery and despair. I'd become a recluse. I would stay holed up in my room for days, even weeks, getting high on cocaine. I lost interest in everything, even the things that used to bring me joy and pleasure.

I was doing so much coke I started to experience bouts of extreme anxiety as well as constant chest pains. With every line, the pain in my chest would get increasingly worse, but I couldn't quit. I couldn't deal with the despondency that ensued once I stopped, so I chose the chest pain and anxiety instead. The anxiety kept building up, and so did the heaviness on my heart. Ultimately, it became too much, and something had to give.

After getting home from the strip club one night after being up for two days, I felt intensely agitated. My chest was hurting so badly I began to get concerned something was seriously wrong. I tried not to do any more drugs that night, but the crash kept pulling me down to the depths of hell, and I would have to do another line to stave it off.

I decided I would just do small lines, but my tolerance was too high at that point. I could feel the demons starting to hover all around me, so, despite the anxiety and chest pain, I snorted a bigger line. That's when a feeling of death reverberated all the way through my body. My chest was pounding, I couldn't breathe, and I honestly thought I was about to experience an overdose again.

I started to panic. I hid my drugs, wiped off my desk, and grabbed my phone and dialed 9-1-1. When the operator answered, I told her I was overdosing on cocaine. When she started asking me questions, I began to second-guess my decision to call 9-1-1. I still thought I was dying, but I also was worried about the police, so I hung up the phone abruptly.

Only minutes after hanging up on the 9-1-1 operator, though, I could see flashlights in my backyard. I went to the back door and met several police officers, including one I knew very well. He was the epitome of what a police officer and civil servant should be. He always seemed to be more interested in helping people than just arresting them or sending them to jail. Despite all my dealings with that specific officer, he always empathized with my situation.

"What's going on, Eric?" the officer asked.

"I mixed a bunch of different pills, and it feels like I'm dying," I replied, not wanting to admit to using a bunch of cocaine.

"OK. Well, an ambulance is on the way. Do you want me to send these other officers away and wait with you?"

"Yes, please. I'd really appreciate that," I answered somberly.

The officer told the other cops to leave, and the two of us sat outside on my deck waiting for the paramedics to arrive. He asked me what type of pills I had consumed, and I told him I wasn't sure, that I just took a bunch of them. I began to cry because I still felt like I was dying, and the officer put his arm around me as I rested my head against his side. He consoled me and reassured me everything would be OK.

When the paramedics showed up and loaded me onto the ambulance, they asked me what was wrong.

Before I answered, I asked, "Does doctor-patient confidentiality apply to you guys as well?"

"Yes, it does," one of the paramedics answered. "Everything you tell us stays between us and the doctors."

"OK. In that case, I've been up for two days doing cocaine, and it feels like I'm overdosing."

"Well, why did you do that?" the paramedic responded, somewhat bewildered.

"Because my life is so fucked up, and I just don't know how to deal with it anymore," I replied as I sat on the stretcher crying my eyes out.

The paramedics inserted an IV and took my vital signs. My blood pressure and heart rate were through the roof, so they gave me a bunch of children's aspirin to chew up and then stuck a nitroglycerin tablet under my tongue. I was given oxygen, and the guys even hooked me up to an EKG monitor. I still thought I might die, but at least I had some confidence the paramedics could possibly revive me if that occurred.

I was admitted to the hospital and had to embarrassingly tell my story to every doctor or nurse who asked me how I ended up there. They ran all sorts of tests on me: bloodwork, another EKG, X-rays, and an ultrasound on my heart. I was expecting the worst news possible, even hoping for it—a damaged heart, narrow arteries, something to motivate me to quit using drugs.

However, when the doctor came in the morning to visit and go over all my test results, he informed me that everything was OK and I had a perfectly healthy heart. I was dumbfounded. All that cocaine, alcohol, and pills, not to mention my paralysis, and he was telling me my heart was completely fine. That was not the news I expected to hear—or wanted to hear, for that matter.

I wanted to stop doing drugs. I wanted the doctor to tell me the next line of cocaine might be my last, that it would kill me. By assuring me my heart was healthy, he was essentially giving me a green light to continue down my destructive path. He gave me a social worker's card, wished me the best, and discharged me from the hospital.

When I arrived home later that day, I still had tightness in my chest and severe anxiety. I should have felt fortunate and lucky, but I was more depressed than ever. I didn't get out of bed or answer my phone for several days. Despite the pure exhaustion, I still had difficulty sleeping. I simply lay in bed contemplating my life and wondering how I had managed to get to such a point of degradation.

For the next week, all I did was reflect on my past life, when things were so perfect. Even though I still had drugs at my house, I had absolutely no desire to use. The mere smell of cocaine would give me a panic attack. There was no longer anything for me to look forward to, not even the euphoria the coke once brought me. I had no silver lining. I was broken, battered, and crestfallen.

One day, I lay awake in bed sobbing uncontrollably and fixating on all the things I missed so badly from before I ended up paralyzed. I missed the way fresh grass and beach sand felt between my toes. I missed those peaceful strolls down a golf course, surrounded by trees while listening to the birds. I missed skiing, lifting weights, and playing softball with the guys. I missed the smell of a beautiful girl lying next to me in bed. Most of all, though, I missed dancing. I missed being at the club and dancing to music, surrounded by the flashing lights. I would never again experience any of those things, so why should I continue living?

As the day went on, I grew more fixated on the negative aspects of my disability and became completely detached from life. The only thing I cared about at that point was my mother. It was her love for me, and my love for her, that kept me going that long. I had great friends whom I loved and cherished deeply, but it was my connection with my mother that gave me purpose. However, not even my mom's unrelenting support and love for me could keep me around any longer.

Besides, the thought of losing her was so unbearable I never wanted to experience that pain—not ever! I figured I might as well be preemptive and avoid that pain along with all the other pain afflicting me over the last few years. Living had officially become unbearable, and it was that very day, while thinking about my mother, that I made the decision to commit suicide, and this time, I meant it.

Later that evening, I dumped all my prescription meds into a bowl and bought a liter of vodka to wash them all down. I had regularly thought about suicide while struggling through cocaine crashes, so I knew exactly how I would do it if I ever decided definitively. Out of all the ways to commit suicide, this was the least violent or traumatic, I felt. I'd simply swallow all my pills, get into bed, and go to sleep—forever.

I knew taking my own life would upset a lot of people, particularly my friends and family, but this was my life. I was the one in so much pain, and not just mental anguish either. I had constant physical pain from dealing with bladder infections, shoulder strains, spasms, muscle aches, nerve pain, and more. I also felt like a tremendous burden to everybody, especially my mom. For that reason alone, I was convinced they'd all be better off without me, and eventually even relieved I was gone.

I took my time that evening. I wrote a suicide letter to explain the reasoning behind my decision. I mixed several drinks, building up some liquid courage, and as I drank my screwdrivers, I searched the internet for subject matter related to heaven, angels, and religion. I was looking for information about the afterlife to help me with the most significant and last decision I was about to make in my physical life.

As I sat in front of my computer reading the internet, I happened upon a link to a song titled, "Angel on my Shoulder," by an artist named Kaskade. I figured it showed up because of the religious information I was Googling, but it still felt rather random. Yearning for a break in the monotony of reading material, I decided to click the link and listen to the song simply out of curiosity.

I pressed play and was slowly mesmerized by the beat and sound. It was music that I had never heard before with lyrics describing my current situation. An angel on my shoulder, the devil in my head—that certainly defined my predicament. Most likely the song was intended to be about love, but song lyrics can reflect many aspects of life. At that specific moment, that song was resonating with me and summed up my life perfectly.

I kept listening, and when the song ended, I searched for more music by Kaskade. I found his album, Strobelite Seduction, released early in 2008, and began listening song by song. Instantly, I was hooked. I was simply captivated by that album and Kaskade's music on the whole. It was so melodic, transcending, and had an electronic sound to it that was so unlike anything I had ever heard before.

I started to remember how happy music used to make me and how much comfort it brought. Early after my accident, it was my only escape, but when my favorite artists began disappearing from the music scene, I became disinterested. Sitting there listening to Kaskade, I realized I should have sought out new music while I was depressed instead of turning to drugs and alcohol.

A couple of hours passed as I sat there on YouTube with music blaring from my computer's sound system. I continued to find similar artists and songs, and I was soon completely obsessed with the genre, which I learned was called EDM (electronic dance music).

It wasn't new music—in fact, its origins date back decades. It was just more underground in its early days. I'm not sure when electronic music started to become more mainstream, but it didn't really matter. I was just thankful that I discovered it that evening and angry I hadn't happened upon it sooner. Better late than never, though, I felt.

Another hour passed as I sat at my desk, and suddenly, it occurred to me that I was no longer drinking, nor was I contemplating suicide. In fact, I was doing the exact opposite. I was smiling, dancing, and thinking positively. My mood and demeanor had shifted entirely—I had done a complete one-eighty. My feelings of hopelessness and despair had completely vanished.

Was this a coincidence? It was another narrow escape from death, thanks to a song that randomly appeared on my computer screen. Suddenly, my life was going in a different direction and had new meaning. Was this a sign from God? It seemed peculiar that I discovered that song while searching for justification to kill myself. Instead, I found a reason to live.

It may sound cliché, but music saved my life that night. More specifically, EDM saved my life. Maybe it wasn't literal, but it definitely breathed new life into me. It gave me something to live for during my darkest moment, and it was the light at the end of the tunnel I was constantly wishing would shine upon me for once. Finally, I had found hope.

I know people will say that my friends and family should have been reason enough to live, but they were no longer able to relieve my pain the way music did the night I decided to end it all. EDM reminded me that life could still be enjoyable and gave me a feeling of happiness that I hadn't felt in years. That music was exactly the detour I needed to steer my life into a more positive and healthy direction.

I stayed awake that night early into the morning, playing music and writing down the names of EDM artists and albums I wanted to purchase. I felt alive for the first time in several years and lost whatever desire I'd had to end my life. I can't say for certain if I would have actually killed myself that night, but I can say the suicide letter was written, emails were sent to my priest, and I was more at peace with the decision than I'd ever been before.

Everything changed that night, though, and for the better. Ironically, the night I decided to end my life was the night I rediscovered it. For the first time in years, I went to bed and fell asleep excited to wake up the next morning. I was so excited, in fact, I kept waking up to write reminder notes about different artists and songs I wanted to search for.

I wanted to listen to more music. I wanted to tell my mom how much I loved her. I wanted to tell my friends how much I appreciated their friendship. More importantly, I wanted a purpose and plan for my life going forward. Not only was I not thinking about death anymore, for the first time since my accident, I truly wanted to live.

V

◆ ◆ ◆ ◆ ◆ ◆ ◆ ◆ ◆

REJUVENATED

CHAPTER TWENTY-FIVE

◆ ◆ ◆ ◆ ◆ ◆ ◆ ◆ ◆

New Beginnings

WITHIN SEVENTY-TWO HOURS, MY life did a complete one-eighty. That Friday, when my supplier came over to pick up his money and drop off more drugs, I told him I was done. I explained how I spent too many nights getting high on my own supply and wasn't making any money dealing drugs. I also told him my heavy use was having an adverse effect on my health, and he completely understood.

From then on, my mornings started off with electronic music blaring from my speakers as I drank a cup of coffee out on my deck. For times when I wasn't at home, I purchased an iPod so I could listen to music on the go. I engulfed myself in music instead of drowning out my sorrows with alcohol and drugs. All that new music brought me so much enjoyment and pleasure, I couldn't stop listening.

I started attending local EDM shows and realized the music was even better live. The events were typically held in a small venue, so it was a very intimate experience. The crowds were always welcoming and inclusive, so it didn't matter who you were. Everybody was accepted regardless of race, religion, sexuality, or even disability. It was all about the music, and the rave scene made me feel young and alive again.

When I attended my first EDM festival, I was truly amazed by the positivity and welcoming environment. It was like the new Woodstock. People were approaching me left and right, happy to see me enjoying life and partaking in such an event despite the obstacles and terrain. They offered to help push me through grass, traded kandi bracelets, bought me drinks, and even more surprisingly, offered me drugs. Not to purchase, either—people were literally offering me free drugs.

If I couldn't see an artist, people would clear a path to the stage. If I needed something, complete strangers would go retrieve it for me. The love and respect being lavished on me was overwhelming. Toward the end of one show, a group of guys offered to lift me up in the air above the crowd in my chair. With all the support and love around me I said why not.

"How much do you weigh with the chair?" some guy asked.

"No more than 175 pounds all together," I replied.

"Shit, that ain't nothing," another guy said. "Hey, J, come help us lift this guy."

"Please, don't drop me," I begged.

"Dude, we got you," a kid reassured me. "Don't worry."

About five guys came over and grabbed ahold of different parts of my chair. All at once, they lifted me straight over their heads and above the fifteen thousand people attending the show. Instantly, the crowd turned my way, cheered, yelled, and applauded my zeal for music and life. I was on cloud nine. Pure, undeniable happiness was all I felt at that moment.

After that festival, I knew music had to be a part of my future in some form. I decided to go back to school and discovered a music production college in Minneapolis while searching online. When I arrived a week later for my visit, I was a little discouraged because the building was old and antiquated—it didn't even have an elevator. They were a private college, so they didn't have to be ADA compliant. I was highly disappointed, and the admissions representative felt bad.

I returned to my search, figuring if I couldn't produce music, then at least I could play music. That's when I decided to get my degree in broadcasting. I found a college that had graduated a long list of famous disc jockeys, and scheduled a visit. During my appointment, the instructors made sure I could access and control the soundboards, and when I got into the studio, I had no problem utilizing the equipment. I was so elated I decided to sign up that same day.

A few weeks later, I returned to the campus to finalize my financial aid and pick up all my required textbooks. My mother was proud of me for going to school and picked me up at the school. When we got back to the house, she came up to put away some groceries she bought for me. The two of us were in the kitchen when the mail carrier knocked on the door with a package that I had to sign for. I thought it was strange the postman was working so late, but I signed for the package without much more thought.

I put the package on the table, and my mother gave me a goodbye kiss on the cheek. I wheeled into my bedroom and excitedly started to tear the shrink-wrap off my text books. That's when I heard a loud banging on my door.

Somebody yelled, "Police!" My friend Billy used to do the same shit, so I figured it was him and disregarded the shouting. However, the knocking and screaming continued.

"Police! Open the door!" More pounding ensued. "Police, search warrant! Open the door!"

"Fuck off, Billy!" I yelled back jokingly.

The next thing I heard was the sound of someone kicking open my door. I wheeled out of my bedroom to investigate, but as I came around the corner, there was a gun pointed directly into my face.

"Don't fucking move!" the officer screamed at me. "Hands in the air!"

I quickly put my hands in the air and pretended I was a statue. I sat there wide-eyed with my jaw on the floor. As the officer started placing handcuffs on my wrists, men with bulletproof vests and assault rifles started pouring through my back door. I looked out the window and saw my backyard was crawling with law enforcement. As more guys with guns gathered in my living room, it seemed like every federal agency with a three-letter abbreviation was in my house, not to mention every local police officer.

Worse yet, my new roommate had just gotten home from work and was in the basement relaxing. He had just started to light up his marijuana pipe when the feds busted open his door. I can't imagine what a surprise that must have been for him. When the agents brought him upstairs, he had the fear of God in his eyes and kept asking me what the fuck was happening. I had asked myself the same question when I saw the gun pointed at me.

It didn't take long for me to figure it out, though. I knew exactly why the feds were there, and it wasn't the coke I used to sell. I had stopped that weeks ago. No, this had to do with the package I had just signed for. The feds, search warrant in hand, were tearing apart my house, but what they were looking for was right on my kitchen table: a box of steroids that I had agreed a while back to let my friend send to my home—correction, my mother's home.

I had been letting him do this for a few months. In exchange, he would pay for a night out at the strip club, bring me bottles of liquor, or throw me some cash here and there. Besides, it was just steroids. Professional athletes got in trouble with steroids all the time, and they never went to jail for it. Who gives a shit about steroids? That was my thought when he first asked if he could send packages to my address.

Apparently, the federal government gave a shit, or else my roommate and I still would have been chilling in our rooms on a beautiful fall evening. Instead, the two of us were handcuffed in my living room being read our Miranda Rights. It all seemed so surreal. I felt like I was on an episode of Cops, and I couldn't stop humming the "Bad Boys" song over again in my head. It wasn't a TV show, unfortunately—it was real life, and I was scared shitless!

The only two guys in my house without guns were standing in my kitchen and appeared to be in charge. I was wheeled into my bedroom by a different agent, and my handcuffs were removed. The two men in charge followed behind us and sat down on my bed directly in front of me. I was still freaking out and in a complete state of panic. I had just completed my financial aid paperwork for school a few hours earlier, and I knew a drug charge would disqualify me from receiving student loans and grants.

"Oh, my God. I can't believe this is happening!" I told them. "I'm supposed to start school next week."

"What are you going to school for?" the lead investigator asked me.

"Radio broadcasting," I replied.

"Why did you choose that?" he asked.

The real reason was my love for music, but I thought I might try to appeal to their sensibility and buy myself some goodwill. I started to rant and lecture them about our federal government's unsustainable fiscal policy and how our trillion dollars in debt and unfunded liabilities were a direct threat to their public pensions. Both were smiling, and then one agent started laughing aloud.

"What's so funny?" one of the men asked the other.

"This is the smartest fucker we've ever put in handcuffs," he replied. Then the two of them both started chuckling at my expense.

After they had their laugh, the lead agent asked me if I had any drugs in the house. I told him I had a little bit of marijuana and the steroids on the kitchen table that I signed for earlier. He told me to go get them both, and like a well-trained dog, I retrieved them as quickly as I could. I wheeled back into my bedroom and gave him the little bag of weed I had and the package that was just delivered.

"What can you tell me about this package, Eric?" the officer said.

"What do you want to know?"

"Let's begin with who it belongs to."

"I'm sure you know the answer to that already."

"Maybe so. I still want you to tell me," he demanded.

"I'll tell you. I told my friend I would never take the fall for his shit. However, I still would like to call my attorney first, if you don't mind?" I asked the investigator.

The federal agent asked me the name of my lawyer, and I gave him Chris's name. Surprisingly, he told me he knew Chris personally and to go ahead and give him a call. Unfortunately, I couldn't get in touch with Chris, so I frantically called John's cell phone. Thankfully John answered, and I explained to him everything that was happening.

While I was on the phone with my lawyer, I saw another friend of mine being escorted through my garage door in handcuffs. I totally forgot he was coming by that evening to give me a haircut. As he pulled into my driveway from the alley, he was met by several federal agents with their guns out. They took him out of his truck, cuffed him, and then brought him into my living room and sat him next to my roommate.

I couldn't believe how the situation was escalating, and I pleaded with my attorney to help us. John wanted me to keep my mouth shut and not talk to the investigators, at least until he could negotiate a deal for immunity. That was something I wasn't comfortable doing, however. I told him my two friends were handcuffed in my living room, and I didn't want them going to jail for something they had nothing to do with.

Once my attorney knew the full story and that the package didn't belong to me, he told me to go ahead and answer their questions. He still advised me it was a risk, but it was a risk I was willing to take. The only thing that mattered to me right then was getting my friend and roommate released. John told me to call him ASAP if they took me to jail. Otherwise, he would stop by tomorrow after he got off work.

I wheeled back into my bedroom and gave them the name of my friend whom the package belonged to. The lead investigator asked me several more questions after that. Some I knew the answers to, but most of them I didn't. I gave them honest answers, though. I told my friend if my house ever got raided, I was going to tell the police who the steroids belonged to, and he told me he fully expected me to do so.

After the interrogation was finished, I asked the feds what would happen next. They told me that it was an ongoing investigation and that I couldn't say anything to my friend. If I did, they told me I would be charged with obstruction, conspiracy, possession, and a whole bunch of other federal charges. I didn't like the idea of lying to my friend, but what choice did I have? They were his steroids, and this was the federal government I was up against. They don't lose in court.

I agreed to keep my mouth shut, but what about the numerous police officers and feds roaming around my yard with guns? I told them word would spread fast! They had no idea about the sophisticated gossip mill that permeated through White Bear Lake. If Johnny kissed Suzie, the whole fucking town knew about it the next day. The investigator agreed and told me if people inquired, tell them they were looking for a former roommate with outstanding warrants.

The agents started packing up their things and told the officers in my living room to release my friends. The lead investigator informed me he'd be in touch and wished me luck in school. I was relieved that I wasn't going to jail, but I felt terrible about the consequences that awaited my friend. After all the police and feds exited my house, the lead investigator informed me my mother was probably anxious to speak with me. Instantly, chills went running up my spine.

"What? My mom is outside?" I asked, shocked.

"Yeah. We pulled her over as she left the house to make sure she didn't have the package," the investigator explained.

"Oh, my fucking God!" I replied.

"Would you like me to stick around a bit?" The federal agent asked.

"Yes! Please, would you?"

My mother had no idea I nearly committed suicide a few weeks earlier. Hearing she was standing outside the entire time federal agents executed a search warrant in her house made me wish I had. For all she knew, I was still doing drugs, and they were there to arrest me for that. I'm glad the police were still there, because a homicide was about to occur. I might as well have picked up a shovel and dug my own grave. My mother was about to kill me!

As my mom walked through the back door, laser beams were shooting from her eyes and piercing my brain. She stared at me, shaking her head with disappointment and anger. I explained to her that I let my friend mail steroids to the house and that I didn't think it was a big deal. She knew the friend I was talking about and just stood there in silence. The lead investigator, who had stayed behind, told my mom that the feds weren't interested in me, but I wasn't completely out of the woods yet.

He explained to my mother what would happen from that point on and then shook her hand and wished me luck again. Good luck with school or good luck with my mom? I wasn't sure which. Regardless, my mother was livid. She walked through her home, examining the mess the feds had made pulling out drawers and rummaging through closets. The basement was a disaster. My mom offered my roommate cash because she felt so bad, but he refused to accept it.

At the end of it all, my mother was still at a loss for words and told me we'd discuss the incident later. Then she told me to not say anything to my step-dad about what had happened. I told her she didn't need to worry about that. He would have been more upset than my mom, so I wasn't saying shit!

After she left, my roommate and I sat in the kitchen reflecting on the events that had just unfolded. The two of us were still in complete shock, never having experienced anything quite so dramatic before. This was something we only saw on television and in movies.

"Do you want to go to the bar?" my roommate asked. "The cops took all my weed."

"Yeah, let's go," I replied emphatically. "I need a fucking drink— badly!"

CHAPTER TWENTY-SIX

◆ ◆ ◆ ◆ ◆ ◆ ◆ ◆ ◆

Contentment

I STARTED SCHOOL THE WEEK after my house was raided by the feds. It was difficult to feel excited, though, since I still had to lie to my friend constantly about my house being raided. He came over to my home and called frequently, inquiring about his missing package. I kept telling him it never arrived, but when he tracked it online, the post office said it was delivered. He grew increasingly suspicious, but he ultimately trusted me when I said I didn't have it.

After about a month, word finally got back to him that my house had been crawling with law enforcement one day, and he put two and two together. When I came home from school one afternoon, he was there waiting to confront me about it. At first, I denied that it was true, but I finally broke down and admitted to what had happened.

I was extremely upset and started crying, partly because of the stress that had built up from lying, and somewhat because I was relieved he knew. Mostly, though, it was because I was concerned about what might happen to him. For the first time since we became friends, he looked worried and distressed. He kept asking me questions about the raid, almost as if he didn't believe the severity of what had occurred, and we got into an intense argument over the fact I didn't tell him about it.

After that, we never spoke again. I always had a feeling that our little arrangement would ultimately lead to the end of our friendship. I called my lawyer Chris and asked him what was going to happen, and he told me my friend would most likely cooperate and agree to some type of plea bargain. Chris said I may have to give a statement somewhere down the road, but ultimately, I never heard from the feds again. I was officially off the hook.

It felt as if a big weight had been lifted off my shoulders, and from that point on, I focused all my efforts on getting my life back. College was going great, and I was learning so much about copywriting, audio production, operating sound boards, curating playlists, etc. It didn't even feel like school, I was having so much fun. Besides, I was meeting so many amazing people and making new friends.

I started working out at a rehab facility in Minneapolis that had gym equipment accessible to people in wheelchairs. I also started weaning off some of my prescription medication. I was eating healthier foods, sleeping better, and feeling a lot more energetic. I was gaining weight, getting stronger, and gaining back the independence that I had surrendered to my drug use in the past. Overall, I was experiencing a true happiness that I hadn't felt in a long time.

With my newfound confidence and zeal for life on full display, people started to take notice, especially women. Most notable was one girl whom I became good friends with after we met through a mutual friend. Eventually, we began dating and discovered the two of us connected on so many different levels—emotionally, spiritually, and even sexually.

For the first time in what seemed like an eternity, I was sexually active again, and not just once in a while. I was having sex quite frequently, like the days before my accident. Without the excessive drinking, cocaine, and prescription meds, I had no problem getting erections. My libido returned as well, and the sex was very sensuous and pleasurable. Best of all, knowing I could satisfy a woman did wondrous things for my self-esteem.

The biggest change I made, though, was my decision to move out of White Bear Lake and away from the dark cloud that hovered above me there. I wasn't the only one who was making that decision at the time, either. A few of my other friends also moved away from the enablers and constant temptation. Some of them had decided it was time to grow up, and some were just sick and tired of being sick and tired. For me, it was a little bit of both.

Nothing defined a fresh start more than a new home, I concluded. Because I was no longer driving, I decided a move to the city was my best option, so I began searching for apartments in downtown St. Paul. The network of skyways and public transportation would give me so much more freedom and independence, and I always thought it would be cool to live in a high-rise complex.

My current house was not handicap friendly, and during the winter, I was virtually trapped inside. The alley, driveway, sidewalk, deck, and elevator always had to be cleared of snow or else I couldn't go anywhere. Furthermore, my mom and step-dad were expending a lot of time and energy with the upkeep. I felt that with me gone, my mother could finally sell the home and be free of that burden.

I waited until my parents left for Mexico before I finalized my decision to move. I knew my mother would be apprehensive—she was very protective, and I didn't want her to try to talk me out of it. Even though the house was a lot of work, I believed my parents were uncertain of my ability to live alone in the city. Because of this, I was highly motivated to prove moving was the best decision for everybody.

I found a nice high-rise apartment with several amenities downtown and scheduled a visit. It was located right next to a park and surrounded by bars and restaurants, and all of it was connected by skyways. I could go anywhere downtown and never have to go outside. It was the perfect environment for somebody in a wheelchair.

I looked at several different apartments within my price range and felt they all would suit my needs. Before I left, though, the agent wanted to show me one last apartment that had just become available. It was expensive, but she told me I had to see it. It was the only one-bedroom on the very top floor, thirty stories up.

We took the elevator to the penthouse, and when she opened the door to the apartment, my jaw hit the ground. There were floor-to-ceiling windows that wrapped around the entire apartment, and you could see for miles upon miles. The view was absolutely amazing. I had never seen anything like it in my life. I was blown away and knew I had to have it.

I put in an application that day. The management company had certain income requirements, so since I wasn't working at the time, I had to make some fake paystubs to meet their application guidelines. I knew I would have to get creative to pay bills, but there was no way I was letting that apartment slip through my hands. Opportunities to live in a place like that don't come around often, and I was willing to do anything to get it.

The leasing agent called me a few days later and informed me my application was approved, and I was ecstatic. When my parents returned from Mexico and saw the apartment, it was hard for them not to be supportive. Just like me, they were astonished by the expansive views the apartment provided, and they could see the excitement written all over my face. It felt like a new beginning for all of us.

Just when I thought things couldn't get any better, I found out one of my favorite electronic music groups was playing a show in St. Paul. They were called Above & Beyond, and I discovered their music the night I almost took my life. I had been listening to them ever since, and they were easily one of my favorite groups at that time. It was their music, along with Kaskade's, that played such a vital role in turning my life around, and I was extremely excited to see them in person.

My sister accompanied me to the show because she loved dance music as well, so I knew she'd have a good time. It was a smaller venue, and the place was packed. You could feel the energy and positive vibes flowing throughout the venue and being so close to the stage made it much more personal. Once Above & Beyond took the stage, it felt like I was experiencing my own religious rapture.

I had watched YouTube videos of their live shows in the past and knew they always brought a fan on stage to "push the button," as their fans called it. The guys would pause one of their songs right before the drop, grab somebody from the audience, and then let them press the play button on stage. The song would come back on, pyrotechnics would go off, and everybody in attendance would go nuts. I just had to be that person.

I wheeled over to the security guard standing in front of the entrance to backstage.

"Can I please be the one to push the button?" I begged. "Please, please, pick me."

"I don't know, man," the security guard answered. "I don't know how they decide that."

"Well, will you go ask them, please?" I pleaded. "I don't know how much longer I have on this earth, and this would make my life complete."

I definitely played the sympathy card, using my disability as leverage, but I had no shame. I was willing to do anything to get on stage.

"OK, OK, chill out, dude," the security guard told me. "I'll see what I can do."

"Thank you, thank you, thank you!" I exclaimed, hugging him for goodwill.

I wheeled back to the handicap section and continued to watch the show. After a few more songs had played, I felt a tap on my shoulder and turned around to see some guy kneeling beside me with the security guard standing behind him.

"Come with us," the random guy yelled into my ear.

Without a second's hesitation, I followed the two guys up the ramp and down a dark hallway leading to the back of the stage. There were a few steps to get onstage, so a couple more security guards were called over to help carry me up. As soon as they lifted me up, I wanted to rush onstage from the adrenaline coursing through my body, but the guy in charge grabbed my shoulder to stop me.

"Hold on there, buddy," he told me, laughing at my excitement.

"OK, sorry," I replied, grinning from ear to ear.

Giddy with anticipation, I watched Above & Beyond from behind the curtains, goosebumps running up and down my arms. Soon, one of their most popular songs, "Sun & Moon," started to play, and after a minute or so, they paused it right before the big drop.

"OK, go," the guy instructed as the band members waved me over.

I wheeled onto the stage with four thousand people in the audience screaming and cheering me on. I got behind the computer and Pioneer turntables, and Paavo, one of the artists in Above & Beyond, showed me which button to push. I took a deep breath, glanced up at the crowd, and just sat there for a second, relishing in the moment. Then I pushed the play button.

Immediately, the song came back on, along with the lights, as lasers and smoke shot out from the stage. Everybody in attendance was jumping up and down, smiling and singing aloud. I was filled with so much excitement that I couldn't just sit behind the deck, so I wheeled to the front of the stage and started dancing. I couldn't contain my excitement. All I felt was pure, unadulterated elation.

At that moment, I didn't even know I was paralyzed or in a wheelchair. I was completely lost in the music and energy that percolated throughout the venue. That was a feeling that no drug could ever provide, and it was without a doubt the happiest moment of my life. Nothing else mattered in that instant. I had no problems, depression, worries, or pain. It was just me, the music, and four thousand like-minded people cheering me on.

The song began to wind down, so I wheeled to the back of the stage to shake the artists' hands. I wanted to tell them how much their music meant to me, how it literally saved my life. I wanted to thank them for letting me on stage to push the button and for the extreme amount of pleasure and happiness it brought me, but I was at a complete loss for words. I was totally star-struck and could barely speak.

The next morning, I woke up to pictures of me onstage going viral on social media. People were talking about the show online, saying it was one of the best concerts they had ever attended. I had the biggest smile on my face as I called all my friends to tell them about my evening.

Tears of happiness streamed down my face as I relived that moment over again in my head. I was filled with more emotions than it is possible to describe. Ecstasy, euphoria, optimism, exuberance—all of them consumed my mind and body. The night I discovered EDM was truly a turning point, but after getting onstage with one of my favorite musical groups and pushing that button, my outlook on life completely changed for the better once again.

Over the following couple of weeks, I kept reliving that moment on stage and the incredible feeling it gave me. I was glowing inside and out, people could see the happiness encompassing me, and I couldn't stop talking about that experience. The music, crowd, energy, and positive vibes had made it a monumental moment and a true turning point in my life.

A little over thirteen years after breaking my neck and becoming a quadriplegic, I was finally content with my disability. That's how much time it took for me to accept my predicament—thirteen long, agonizing years. I know this because on August 27 of that summer, I completely forgot it was the anniversary of my accident. Every year before that, I'd use that day as an excuse to get drunk and do drugs. In the thirteenth year, however, it was just another day.

People with spinal cord injuries usually say you never accept your disability, you just learn to live with it, but that wasn't true with me. I finally accepted that my life would never be like it was before my accident and that it was time to move on. I knew I could be happy still, even with my paralysis. In fact, after that Above & Beyond show, I realized just how amazing life truly was.

Music played a key role in that acceptance. It reinvigorated my spirit and was the shining light during my darkest days. With music, I realized that life was still very much enjoyable. As long as I had my hearing, I could always listen to music, and as long as I could see, I could still find beauty in this world. Paralysis had robbed me of my body, but it couldn't take my mind.

CHAPTER TWENTY-SEVEN

◆ ◆ ◆ ◆ ◆ ◆ ◆ ◆ ◆

Onward & Upward

AFTER THE ABOVE & BEYOND show, I was riding a wave of positivity that I hadn't experienced since the days before my accident. With all my positivity came increased popularity, particularly with the ladies. I was meeting a lot of girls at the EDM shows I attended, and I received numerous friend requests on Facebook from random women. Of course, I always accepted their requests and was friendly and flirtatious—all to my girlfriend's chagrin, of course.

From then on, my relationship with my girlfriend became very combative. She persistently accused me of cheating on her, and we constantly argued about my new friendships. Truthfully, I was always loyal to her, but she never believed me. Every time a girl said hi to me in public or on social media, she would fly into a fit of rage. In my view, blood would pour from her eyes and her head would start spinning around, just like the girl from The Exorcist.

Beautiful women had always been my kryptonite. This fact never changed, even after my accident. My girlfriend always gave me ultimatums, but I just couldn't resist all the temptation. While she wanted to settle down and start a family, all I wanted to do was bask in my newfound attention. I felt like I had rediscovered my youth and just wanted to let loose and be free. I wasn't going to stop talking and hanging out with other girls that I'd become friends with, and she couldn't accept that—or trust me, for that matter. Ultimately, that was our undoing.

Nonetheless, I owe that girl more than she'll ever realize. During our brief relationship and time together, she played a vital and instrumental role in helping me turn my life around. She gave me the confidence I needed to have sex again. It was because of her that I realized I could satisfy women sexually. That type of self-confidence had vanished from my life for so many years, and she made it reappear.

The manner in which our relationship ended was sad, but in the end, I believed it was the best decision for both of us. She could now seek out what she truly wanted in life, and I could focus on graduating college, meeting new people, and capitalizing on the positive steps I was making in rebuilding my life. Having a girlfriend was great for a short while, but the constant fighting had become an obstacle to my self-betterment.

I continued to move onward and upward, and I finally finished college. When graduation day arrived, it was truly a tremendous achievement in my life. Throughout my nearly two years in college, I was able to live on my own, pay rent, and make it to class every day despite my disability. All the while, I maintained a 3.45 GPA, just short of graduating with honors but still something to be extremely proud of given the obstacles in my life.

Receiving my diploma that day was almost as gratifying as being on stage with Above & Beyond. My father even surprised me by showing up to my graduation, and I was so happy to see him. Even though he had been absent during my toughest times, I had no bitter feelings. He had spent that time fixing his own problems, just like I was trying to fix mine. I was simply glad he had finally found happiness again, just like I had.

After graduation, I went to work finding a job in broadcasting. Unfortunately, the jobs for new graduates were located out of state or in small rural towns hours away. Because of my disability and the support system I had in place, I just didn't have the luxury of being able to move away. As a result, I couldn't secure a job in broadcasting in my city despite applying for countless positions.

Regardless, I wouldn't have moved even if I could. Being a famous DJ would be great, but not as great as all my friends and family. No amount of money or material possessions was more valuable than the love I had from my family and friends. Next to music, they were the most important things in my life, and I would never want to be apart from them.

With that said, I still needed to find a job, and fast. Rent in a penthouse apartment in the heart of the city isn't cheap, and there were no more savings or student loans for me to draw upon. I wanted to maintain my standard of living, and a job was necessary for my mental health as well. My mother was very helpful financially; however, I didn't want to rely on her for money, so I took a job at the first place that I could.

Since I had over a decade's worth of experience in financial services, I applied for and accepted a position with another big bank located a short distance from my apartment. The position paid well and had great benefits, and it was a very positive work environment. I had an awesome manager who taught me a lot about sales, and I ended up becoming good friends with a few of my co-workers.

Even though it wasn't a job working in radio, I was still very proud of all my accomplishments up to that point. After everything I endured over the years, I had graduated college, landed a good job with a Fortune 500 company, and stayed away from the hard drugs that nearly drove me to commit suicide. With all the obstacles thrown in front of me, those milestones were still rather gratifying.

After a little more than a year working at the bank, I had several setbacks, mostly related to my health, and I unfortunately had no choice but to quit my job. I had a couple of bouts of sepsis that nearly killed me, rotator cuff surgery, and a neck fusion that permanently damaged my vocal chords. At the same time, I lost my dear friend and attorney John to cancer.

I'm not going to lie—I became overwhelmed, and there were a few times I just wanted to bury my face in a pile of cocaine and drown my struggles and sorrows in drugs like I had in the past. However, I remained steadfast and reminded myself how those short-term solutions may seem justifiable when I felt broken, but they would only lead to more long-term problems. I had thirteen years of soul-crushing life lessons to reference, and because of that, it took me all of thirteen seconds to know cocaine and booze were not viable solutions.

I knew what I needed to do to get through the surgeries, infections, and mental fatigue. Whenever I felt downtrodden, I simply recalled what stopped me from killing myself a few years earlier and sought out music as my refuge and escape. Whether it was attending a concert or blasting music through the sound system in my apartment, music continued to give me the spark to get through the tough times and on to the next day.

Music always did the trick. Not only was it my new stimulant of choice, it became my medicine as well. The concerts were my hospital, the DJs my doctors, and my fellow ravers the nursing staff. Add my friends and family to the mix, and it all became my fountain of youth. I felt like I was twenty years old, and most of the time, I acted like it.

I know many of my longtime friends and high school buddies don't understand my love of EDM and my attachment to the concerts and festivals I frequent. Quite frankly, it's hard to explain my adoration when they ask me about it. All I know is when I'm at a show sitting amidst the crowd, I periodically just stop, smile, and absorb everything happening around me because it still seems so surreal.

The lights, music, energy, positivity, and being surrounded by people dancing to music we all love and relish in—I just stop and think to myself, This is happiness. That's what happiness feels like to me, and sometimes I just sit there smiling. I may look completely lost, but I'm not. I'm right where I want to be—where I need to be— and my wheelchair becomes nonexistent, as does my paralysis.

Several years after my accident, one of my good friends purchased the house on White Bear Lake where my accident occurred. He regularly held gatherings and barbecues, inviting our friends over there to party, but I repeatedly declined his invites to join them. I was always afraid of the memories going over to that house would conjure up. Returning to the place where my perfect life was destroyed just seemed too unbearable.

However, after I turned my life around and found contentment and peace of mind about my disability, I said screw it and attended one of his parties. That night, I sat on his deck watching the sun set on the lake, drinking, laughing, and having a great time with the same friends who were there twenty years earlier on the night I became a quadriplegic.

Somehow, I wasn't dwelling on or even thinking about my accident. Directly behind me was the retaining wall I dove off when I broke my neck. I stared at it briefly, but I felt no emotion. After all those years, it had become nothing more than a fixture on the property. What I was focused on was how much fun I was having, how it was such a beautiful night to be on the lake around such great friends, and what an amazing life I had. At that moment, everything felt perfect again.

EPILOGUE

◆ ◆ ◆ ◆ ◆ ◆ ◆ ◆ ◆

DO NOT WASTE

IRONICALLY, AFTER EVERYTHING I SUFFERED, fought through, and learned over all the years since my accident, my life has come full circle, all the way back to when I was a little kid in the car with my father after my soccer game. He had warned me about wasted talent, almost as if he had a crystal ball and could foretell my future.

Obviously, becoming a quadriplegic had devastating consequences for me. I spent the decade after my accident drinking and doing cocaine, trying to drown out my sorrows. I sunk so low and did so many drugs that eventually I almost committed suicide. When I finally came to my senses, so much of my life—so many days, weeks, months, and years—had been completely wasted. I wasted time, I wasted talent, I wasted relationships, and I wasted money.

While doing some research for this book, I looked at past bank statements and did some math. After checking over my numbers several times, I concluded that I spent at least a hundred thousand dollars on cocaine over those ten to twelve years. I conferred with some of my friends who were in that circle of users, and we concluded that between us all, we easily spent a million dollars on drugs—and that's a conservative estimate. Talk about waste.

It's not just the money, either—it's all that time I'll never get back. Sure, we had a lot of fun times and great parties. Toward the end, though, we became hermits locked away in our houses, peering out the blinds, too paranoid and fucked up to step out into society. I spent so much time sitting at my desk or lying in bed thinking about deep, dark, depressing shit. That's time I'll never get back, and it angers me knowing all the productive things I could have done instead.

Nowadays I often read stories about somebody sustaining a spinal cord injury and then going on to start some charity or nonprofit that assists others with disabilities. Surprisingly, they do it within a couple of years after their accident. I know quadriplegics who have gone on to become lawyers and engineers, even getting their master's degree or PhD. I know of quadriplegics who can't even move their arms, so they learned to paint with their mouths and became talented artists.

I have so much admiration and respect for those individuals. Instead of wasting their time wallowing in their misery, they went on to start organizations or careers doing something noble. Their losses were just as significant as mine, regardless of how much more athletic or gifted I thought I was. Furthermore, many other quadriplegics are much worse off physically than I am, so paralysis should have been easier for me to handle than it was for many of them.

Looking back at everything I did over those twelve years or so—all the sad events and stories of drug and alcohol abuse—is certainly difficult to accept. I wish I could go back in time and do things over, but I can't. Like the saying goes, hindsight is always 20/20. Music showed me I could still find happiness in life, and I'm disappointed I couldn't come to that realization much sooner.

Furthermore, there are so many people in this world who have it much worse off than I do. When I start to compare my situation to theirs, I begin to count my blessings and appreciate my life so much more, and spend less time feeling sorry for myself because I was paralyzed. All that time, I should have been thankful I wasn't dead and relieved I could still do so many things despite my disability.

We are only given one chance at life, one opportunity to live on this planet and participate in the wonders of our tiny world. Life is so fragile and delicate, I learned. Nobody is promised or guaranteed safety, good health, success, or a life free of pain or tragedy. I could have easily died the night of my accident or the morning I overdosed, but I was given a second chance, and I'm so thankful for that now.

When I rediscovered happiness and an appreciation for life through music, I was ultimately left with a simple choice: I could either continue down the path of self-destruction, feeling depressed about my disability, or I could figure out a way to handle my unfortunate circumstance and move forward. I should have been concentrating what I could do, not what I couldn't do.

If you or a loved one is struggling with a condition that affects your physical abilities but you still have your mind and senses, you are still capable of doing great things in this world. Just look at Stephen Hawking. ALS completely took that man's physical ability, but by working out complicated mathematical equations, he solved the mysteries of black holes and the workings of our universe, becoming one of the most respected scientists of our time. He did all of this by controlling a computer with his eyeball.

After my accident, I wasted my time and talent locked away in my house, consuming drugs and alcohol because I was depressed. As a result, I never accomplished anything significant. I distressed the people around me who loved and cared for me, and I nearly took my own life. I'm glad I didn't, because I appreciate my life so much now despite my wheelchair and limitations.

When I dove into that water, broke my neck, and woke up in the hospital paralyzed, I was not prepared mentally for such a profound loss. The joy I derived from living was, for the most part, directly related to my physical capabilities. When I lost my physicality due to my spinal cord injury, I just assumed my life was over. I was so superficial I never grasped the power of my mind.

Trying to drown out your sorrows or escape your past with drugs and alcohol will only bring you more pain and misery. Conquering your demons and discovering what makes you happy will rejuvenate your spirit and make you feel alive again. Even though I could have died the night of my accident, my life didn't end after becoming a quadriplegic. In actuality, it had only just begun.

I wish it hadn't taken me so long to realize how great my life still was despite my loss, but hopefully others in similar predicaments will learn from my mistakes. People need to understand it's OK to not be OK. I'm such a better human being for what I've had to endure, so much more enlightened. I can say with some degree of certainty that if I was offered my body back in exchange for what I've learned about love and life since my accident, I don't think I'd make that deal now.

I believe life is worth living, regardless of the hardships we must face. In my opinion, there is no meaning to life—it is simply God's gift to us, if you believe that. And if you don't, there's no denying the sanctity of life, even if you believe human beings are the byproduct of microbial life, luck, and millions of years. The wonderment and immense complexities in that process are still beyond amazing. I guess my point is this: we're all lucky to be here, so cherish every moment you're alive.

Remember that it is during our most challenging and darkest moments that we must never stop searching for that enduring light. Because in that light is where we find life, and life is worth living and fighting for no matter the obstacles in our path. Do not, under any circumstances, take it for granted. Keep pushing on. It's worth it—I promise.

Nobody truly knows what waits for us when our time on earth is finally up, so don't waste a precious second dwelling on past mistakes or negativity. Appreciate your friends, love your family, discover what makes you happy, and live every day to the fullest.

Finally, I share the words of one of my favorite EDM artists, Avicci. His music brought me so much joy, and his early death brought me profound sadness. He wrote: "One day you'll leave this world behind, so live a life you will remember." I know I will, and I hope that those who read my story will do the same.

ACKNOWLEDGEMENTS

◆ ◆ ◆ ◆ ◆ ◆ ◆ ◆ ◆

FIRST AND FOREMOST, I WOULD like to give thanks to my mother for her unrelenting love and support throughout all these difficult years. You are my sun, my energy, my motivation to never give up. My entire world revolves around you, and like Earth without the sun, I could not live without you in my life. I love and cherish you beyond words. Secondly, I'd like to give special thanks and my heartfelt appreciation to my editors Elizabeth Buege and Jaime Lea. Without your guidance and expertise my story would've never come to fruition. You helped me turn a bunch of words into a real book and genuine story, and I'm forever grateful. Thirdly, thank you to Kaskade (Ryan Raddon), for saving me and inspiring me to live with your music when I truly thought all hope was lost, and to the group Above & Beyond for allowing me to push the button that further reset my life.

The same goes to all the artists, producers, and musicians, that fill this world with transcending sounds and beautiful melodies that brighten our every day. To the doctors, therapists, nurses, and other healthcare related workers, thank you for fixing my broken body and nursing me back to health. Your contributions to society are incomprehensible. To my attorneys Chris and John, thank you for your legal expertise, guidance, friendship, empathy and valuable service. John, may you rest in peace. You will always be missed and never forgotten. Finally, thank you to my family members and close friends that stuck by my side and never gave up on me. You all truly make life worth living, and I love and value our relationships more than words could ever describe. And thank you to all those that read this book and took an interest in my story. All this hard work would've been meaningless without your interest and attention. I love you all. Sincerely, thank you, everybody.

ABOUT THE AUTHOR

◆ ◆ ◆ ◆ ◆ ◆ ◆ ◆ ◆

ERIC ANDERSON IS AN ASPIRING author and entrepreneur. He lives in Saint Paul, Minnesota, with his very loud and obnoxious cat named Sebastian. Eric considers himself a minimalist and prefers gaining new adventures and life experiences as opposed to material possessions. He takes pleasure in the simple things in life such as, sushi, a glass of wine, music, and the feeling of the warm sun shining upon his smiling face. After a disabling accident at an early age, Eric had to endure and overcome many hardships in life, and now lives every moment to the fullest. Most of his spare time is spent attending concerts and music festivals in his city or across the country, where he enjoys meeting new and exciting people. Eric has been told his annoying youthfulness is getting old, but he takes that as a compliment. He values his friends and family members the most, and believes strongly in positive thinking, meditation, and deep thought. By doing so, anyone can make their dreams reality.

CPSIA information can be obtained
at www.ICGtesting.com
Printed in the USA
LVHW060812280419
615812LV00009B/146/P

9 780578 482453